Home Quilt Home

Home Quilt Home

Janet Clare

David and Charles

www.stitchcraftcreate.co.uk

CONTENTS

WELCOME

I love houses. I love everything about them — from looking around friends' homes, visiting stately mansions on holiday, and browsing the estate agents windows in town, to walking around villages admiring the pretty cottages. I love them because houses very quietly but eloquently tell the story of who lives there, and I really find that fascinating.

So, researching and creating this book full of houses and quilts, which are two of my very favourite things, has been a real treat. I spent days daydreaming about living in lighthouses, what winters would be like living in windswept cottages on the moors or leading a busy life bustling about in a neat town house. I could spend an hour looking at mansions online and call it 'research' and daydream to my heart's content whilst drawing a row of beach huts.

I had such fun and I think it shows. I hope I've created a happy and warm book full of projects you'll enjoy making as much as I did. Please feel free to use my designs as starting points, to mix and match the templates, to add more colour, to change the scale – everything is versatile. Make the quilt *you* want to make.

And yes, these quilts will take you hours to make, but they will all be happy ones. And where's the hurry anyway? Enjoy the process: put on your favourite songs, make a cup of tea and just be glad to be creating. All the hours you invest in creating these textile treasures will not be wasted – you will see and feel them every time you enjoy using what you have made. You will remember where you sat and embroidered, the dress the patch came from, laughing whilst stitching the binding on. You're not only making a quilt, you are piecing memories together too, which will add comfort to any room – even those far from home.

I've never met a single soul who on being given a quilt complained about a wonky hem or a mismatched seam so please stop pointing out all your little sewing mistakes. You know you do it! Simply smile and accept the compliments graciously. Remember, you have created a quilt full of warmth, colour, texture and comfort and the rest can safely be forgotten.

And lastly, please don't keep your quilts 'for best'. Every quilt aspires to be well-worn, frayed, faded and loved. So use them, wash them, build dens with them, take them on picnics, sleep under them, wrap up and watch the sunset in them, put your babies on them, spill wine on them. Really *live* with your quilts and they will absorb the very essence of your home and life. If the stitching comes undone stitch it back together or add a patch to it. Think of it as adding another memory.

It has been a real pleasure creating this book and I'd like to thank you for your kind interest in my work. I hope I have inspired you to create a house-filled quilt for your home. Remember, whether you're in the town, country or at the coast, you are always at home with a quilt.

HOME

A valued place offering security and happiness, regarded as a refuge or place of origin.

MEASUREMENTS

All of the projects in this book were made using Imperial inches and although metric conversions have been given in brackets the most accurate results will be obtained using inches.

RULERS AND ROTARY CUTTERS

Traditionally, quilters cut their fabric with scissors and of course you can still do that if you wish. I do still use a tape measure and ruler from time to time. However, using a rotary cutter, a self-healing cutting mat and a large acrylic ruler will increase your speed and accuracy when cutting and measuring fabric.

SCISSORS

You will need at least a couple of pairs of scissors – a large pair for cutting lengths of fabric and a small, sharp pair for cutting out small details and fiddly bits. I also keep a pair of scissors just for paper and cutting fusible web.

PINS AND NEEDLES

Quilters are surprisingly fussy about the pins they use! I like to use Clover flat-headed pins, which are very sharp and long. You can also use them with your quilter's ruler and rotary cutter as they lay completely flat in the fabric. You will find it useful to have a wide range of sewing and quilting needles. I'm not loyal to any brand, but I like them to be sharp so I replace them regularly. If you keep your pins and needles in a pincushion filled with sand it helps to keep them sharp.

MACHINE NEEDLES

You need a new, very sharp needle for free-machine stitching. Did you know you're supposed to change your sewing machine needle after every five hours of sewing time? For my work I use denim needles (size 80/12), which have sharp points and a strong shank designed for stitching through many layers of fabric.

SAFETY PINS

I use curved safety pins to keep my quilt layers together whilst I am quilting them. You will need a surprisingly large number of them.

IRON AND IRONING BOARD

Quilters iron, or more accurately *press*, their fabric constantly. Funnily enough this sort of ironing is not a chore, whereas doing the work shirts really is! Some quilters prefer to use a dry iron, but I'm happy to use my steam iron.

SEWING MACHINE

I use Pfaff sewing machines. I have a Quilt Expression 4.0 and a slightly more basic 2044. If you are looking for a new sewing machine for quilting you would do well to look for one with a long and high throat, which allows plenty of room for your quilt roll when you are machine quilting. You will also want to be able to lower the feed dogs and have a darning foot attachment. Anything else is an asset but not essential for my patchwork and quilting techniques.

MARKING TOOLS

There are lots of marking tools available. I mainly use a water-soluble fabric pen but you could use a pencil for light fabrics or chalk for dark fabrics.

THREADS

I prefer to use a Gütermann polyester thread for my free-machine drawing technique. Polyester does not snap or fray as readily as cotton thread, so it is much kinder to you when you are drawing with your sewing machine. I don't like black as I feel it has a deadening effect so I use a deep charcoal (shade 701) for most of my free-machine drawing. For piecing I like shade 633, which is a neutral dust colour.

FABRICS

Traditionally, quilters saved and used any scrap of fabric they could find, and I think that is still a lovely way to create quilts. Gather good quality wool, cotton and linen fabrics from charity shops (thrift stores). If you pretend they are a haberdashery store you will look at their rails very differently – buttons can be cut off shirts, ties are beautifully printed silk – simply shop with your imagination! It is perhaps more practical, however, to buy 100% cotton patchwork fabric, which comes in thousands of wonderful designs and colour coordinated collections and is of excellent quality.

Fabric stash

Every real quilter has a bigger fabric stash than they care to admit to! I keep even the smallest scrap too, as they might come in handy one day. I've given up trying to organize my fabric – I just throw it in drawers and boxes and hope for the best!

Right sides and wrong sides

The right side of the fabric is the one where the pretty design looks the best. However, I often use the *wrong* side to create muted colours and tonal effects in my quilts. If you use the front and the back of a print in the same quilt it will look aged and vintage.

The selvedge

Patchwork fabric has a fine, even weave that holds its shape when cut and does not fray too much. The warp threads run vertically the length of the fabric and the weft threads run across from side to side. Where these weft threads wrap round the warp threads at the edges is called the selvedge. The selvedge will be printed with the name of the fabric company and will also have little dots of colour on it – one dot for every colour and tone used in the fabric. Keep the selvedges in your purse so you will be able to match threads and find coordinating fabrics easily without carrying yards of fabric with you everywhere.

WADDING (BATTING)

I like to use 100% Quilter's Dream Cotton wadding, which is 120in (305cm) wide and does not require pre-washing. This wadding is low loft (thin) and is very well behaved and easy to work with.

FUSIBLE WEB

Fusible web works just like double-sided adhesive tape, but for fabric. You can stick any shape of fabric to another by ironing, which melts the glue of the web. There are many brands available but the one I use is Bondaweb (also called Vliesofix and Wonder-Under). It has a paper side that you can draw on and trace templates through and can be bought by the metre. Store it rolled to prevent the layers separating.

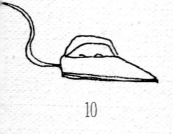

I'm at my happiest and most comfortable whilst sewing when I have my favourite apron on, the radio tuned to BBC Radio 4, a cup of tea (or glass of wine) by my side with a slice of cake or some chocolate to keep my strength up.

NEAT TOWN HOUSES QUILT

I'm sure many of you live in a street like this – rows and rows of nearly identical houses, all uniformly neat and tidy. I enjoyed adding the appliqué numbers to all of the houses in this quilt and loved the graphic simplicity of them against the grey houses.

It could be fun to make the appliqué house with the same number as your actual home really stand out. Or why not make a quilt for a house-warming gift and add an embroidered date on it? I hope you have fun making your rows of neat houses!

Requirements

Fabric for wholecloth background 1½yd/m

Selection of greys, dark grey and red fabrics for appliqué motifs (houses 6in x 4½in/15.2cm x 11.4cm)

Backing fabric 1½yd/m

Binding fabric ½yd/m

Wadding (batting) 40in x 49in (102cm x 125cm)

Fusible web 1yd/m

Polyester sewing thread: dark grey and red for free-motion stitching

Cream machine quilting thread

Finished size: 36in x 45in (91.4cm x 114.3cm)

Templates needed: two house templates, numbers 0–9 (reversed, ready to use)

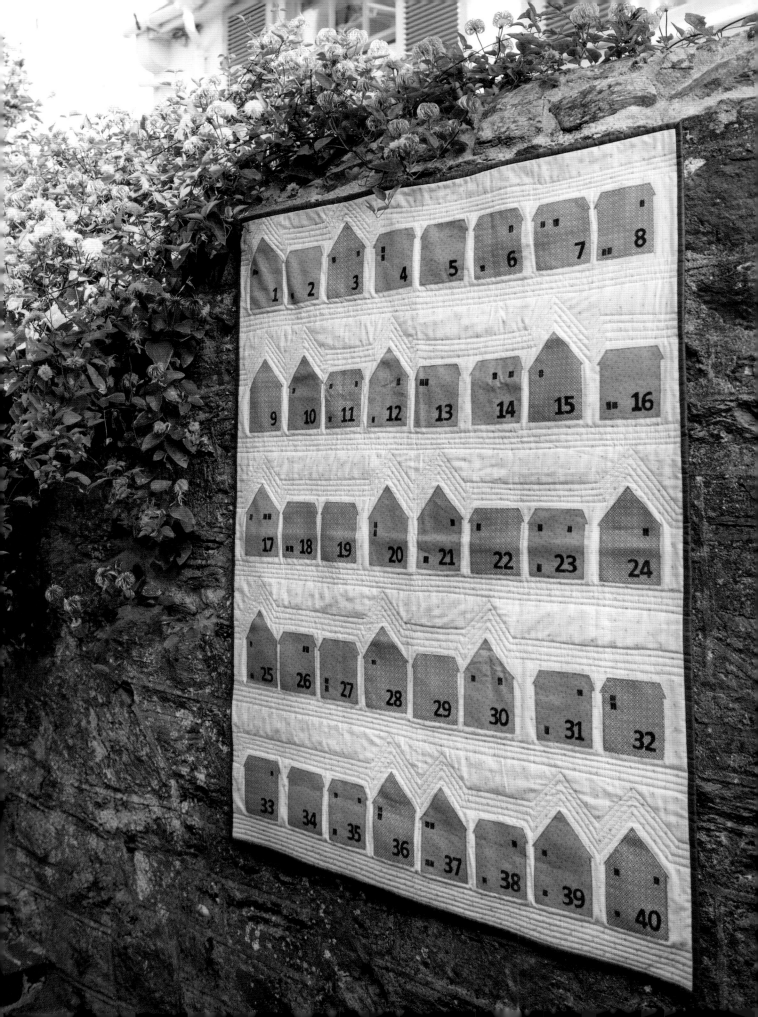

INSTRUCTIONS

1 Prepare fabrics: Wash and press all your fabrics before you start. Trim the wholecloth fabric background to size after careful pressing.

2 Prepare the appliqués: Use the templates provided in the Templates section to create your own houses. I made two templates – one with a flat roof and one with a pointed roof. Use two different fabrics for the houses and the red fabric for the numbers and prepare the appliqués following the instructions in Techniques: Fusible Web Appliqué. Arrange all your appliqué pieces very carefully on the background

fabric as once they are pressed in place with the iron they cannot be removed. Fuse the houses into place and then position and fuse all the numbers.

3 Stitch the appliqués: Set your sewing machine up for free-motion quilting and using a contrasting thread, stitch around the houses and windows. Now change your thread colour and stitch the numbers one at a time. Try to be confident – go on, you can do it! For more guidance on this see Techniques: Free-Motion Quilting.

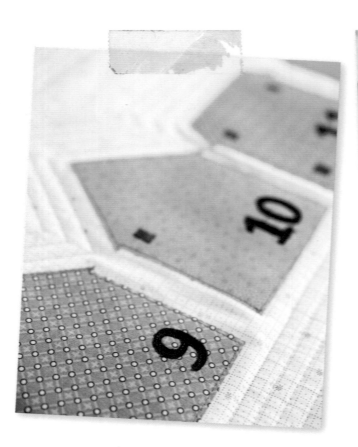

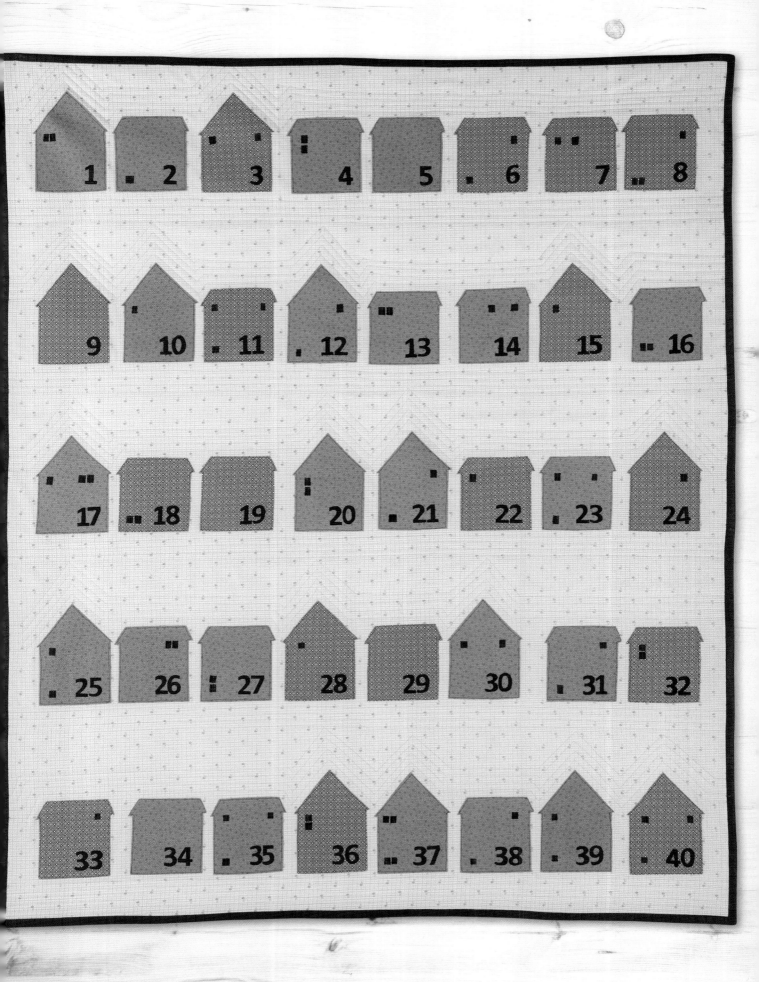

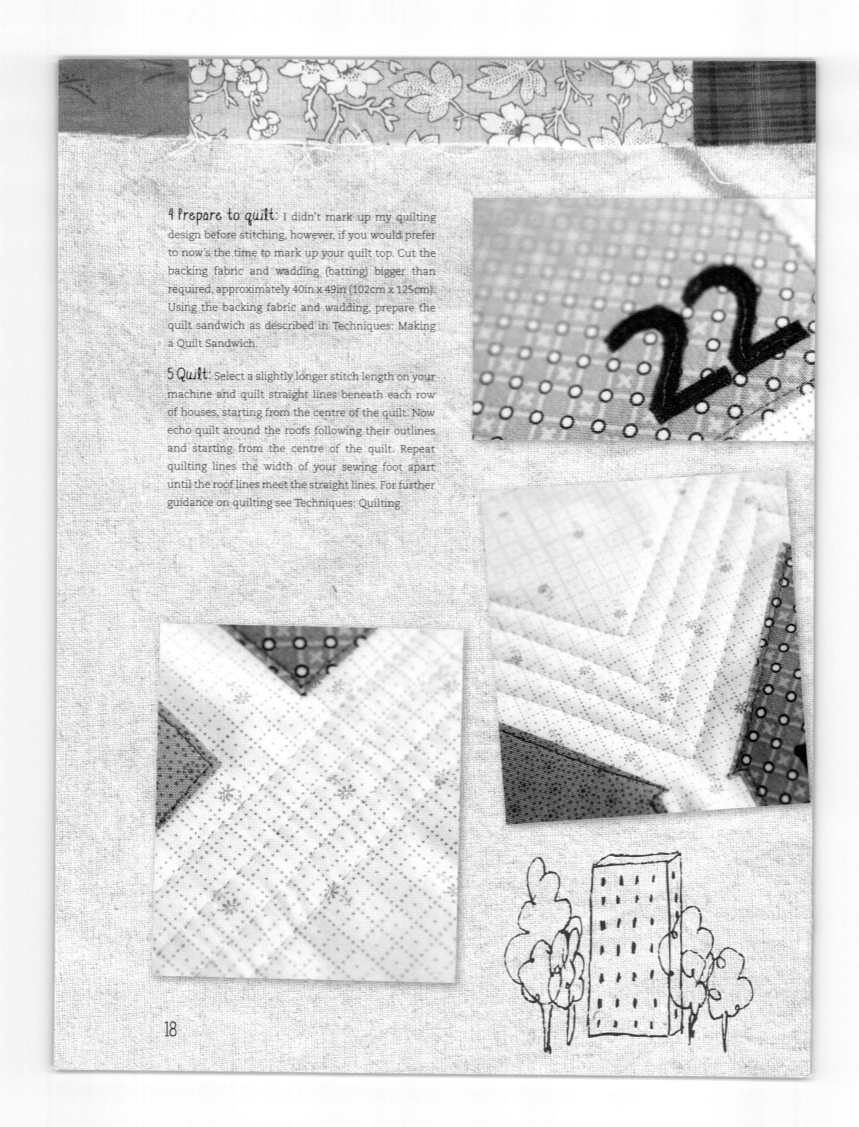

4 Prepare to quilt: I didn't mark up my quilting design before stitching, however, if you would prefer to now's the time to mark up your quilt top. Cut the backing fabric and wadding (batting) bigger than required, approximately 40in x 49in (102cm x 125cm). Using the backing fabric and wadding, prepare the quilt sandwich as described in Techniques: Making a Quilt Sandwich.

5 Quilt: Select a slightly longer stitch length on your machine and quilt straight lines beneath each row of houses, starting from the centre of the quilt. Now echo quilt around the roofs following their outlines and starting from the centre of the quilt. Repeat quilting lines the width of your sewing foot apart until the roof lines meet the straight lines. For further guidance on quilting see Techniques: Quilting.

6 Bind the quilt: Check your quilt is straight and the right size, trimming if necessary. Prepare sufficient binding to go around your quilt, plus about 8in (20cm). Refer to Techniques: Binding. Now sew the binding in place all around your quilt – see Techniques: Stitching the Binding for details.

7 Finish off: All quilts deserve a label, which should include your name and the date the quilt was finished. You could embroider directly onto the quilt or make a little patch of fabric to slipstitch in place – see Techniques: Labelling a Quilt. Once finished, show your lovely quilt off to everyone!

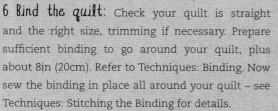

STREET SKYLINE QUILT

For this quilt I thought it would be fun for you to play at being an architect or a town planner and design your own houses, so I drew various houses, roofs and chimneys for you to mix and match. Everyone needs to stamp their individuality on their home when their neighbour's house is identical. Now go and make a quilt that celebrates life in town!

Requirements

Grey fabric for background 2yd/m
Cream fabric for appliqué houses 1yd/m
Assorted fabrics for four striped rows each 6½in x 60½in (16.5cm x 153.7cm) – made up of 2½in wide strips
Backing fabric 4yd (3.75m)
Binding fabric ¾yd/m
Wadding (batting) 64in (163cm) square
Fusible web 2yd/m
Beige machine quilting thread

Finished size: 60in (152.5cm) square

Templates needed: various house parts to create your own houses

INSTRUCTIONS

1 Prepare fabrics: Wash and press all your fabrics before you start. Cut three 12½in x 60½in (31.8cm x 153.7cm) grey rectangles for the appliqué backgrounds. Cut sufficient 2½in (6.3cm) wide scraps of any length to piece the striped patchwork rows. You will need strips totalling a minimum of 720in (1829cm) or 20yd (18.25m).

2 Chain piece the patchwork rows: Arrange your fabric into piles but don't worry about sorting the colours. Chain piece these together on the sewing machine, stitching pairs right sides together. Don't cut the thread when you reach the end of your seam, simply keep the machine running and slowly insert the next pair of fabrics to be sewn together – you will end up with pairs of fabrics sewn together like bunting. Snip the threads between the pairs and then repeat the process, so that you are sewing the pairs

into fours and so on. Repeat until you have lengths of fabric measuring a minimum of 60½in (153.7cm) long. Press all seams.

3 Stitch the rows together: Once you have chain pieced your lengths of fabric you can sew three of them together to form a 6½in x 60½in (16.5cm x 153.7cm) striped row. Make three more the same. Press the work.

4 Prepare the appliqué: Use the templates provided in the Templates section to create your own houses, tracing some of them very close together to form a skyline effect. Prepare the appliqués following the instructions in Techniques: Fusible Web Appliqué. Arrange all your appliqué pieces very carefully on the background fabric 2¼in (5.7cm) from the bottom of the fabric. Once the appliqué is pressed in place with the iron it cannot be removed.

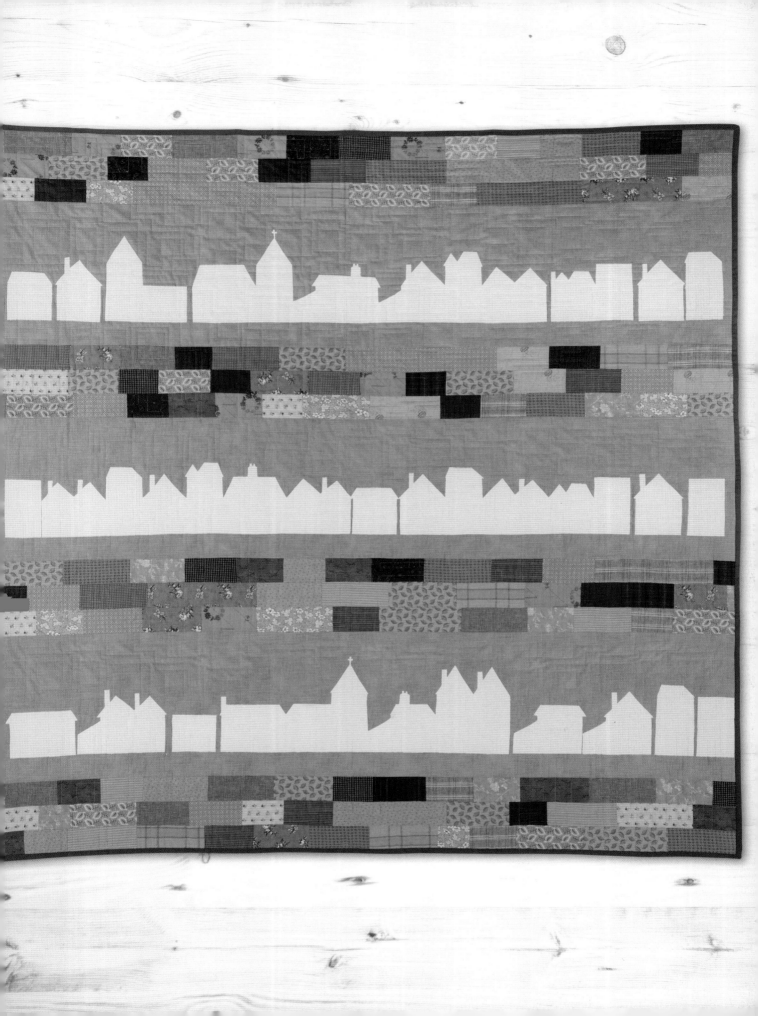

5 Stitch the quilt backing: This quilt is large so you will need to piece the backing fabric together neatly first. Cut the backing fabric in half so you have two pieces approximately 42in x 72in (107cm x 183cm). Sew the pieces back together side by side so you have a backing approximately 84in x 72in (213cm x 189cm). Press the seam open.

6 Prepare to quilt: Cut the backing fabric and wadding bigger than required, approximately 64in (162.6cm) square. Using the backing fabric and wadding (batting), prepare the quilt sandwich as described in Techniques: Making a Quilt Sandwich.

7 Quilt: The machine quilting will secure the appliqué to the background so it is vital that the design is closely worked. I sent my quilt away to be long-armed with a geometric design that mimics a street map. You could create a similar pattern using Fig 1 as a guide. The quilt can also be machine quilted at home with straight horizontal or vertical lines stitched closely together. Select a slightly longer stitch length on your machine and quilt straight lines starting from the centre of the quilt and working out. For further guidance on quilting see Techniques: Quilting.

8 Bind the quilt: Check your quilt is straight and the right size, trimming if necessary. Prepare sufficient binding to go around your quilt, plus about 8in (20cm). If necessary, refer to Techniques: Binding. Now sew the binding in place all around your quilt – see Techniques: Stitching the Binding for details.

9 Finish off: All quilts deserve a label, which should include your name and the date the quilt was finished. You could embroider directly onto the quilt or make a little patch of fabric to slipstitch in place – see Techniques: Labelling a Quilt.

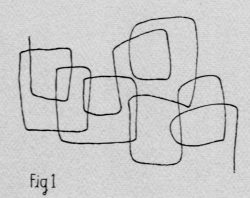

Fig 1

BUSY TOWN WALL HANGING

Now this wall hanging was really good fun to stitch! How you approach this project is up to you — you could let your imagination do the work and stitch any shape of house you dream up, or you could look at the property pages of a newspaper and copy the houses there.

All you really need to start is confidence and a pieced background cloth. So, start drawing the house from the top left and work across the pieced background, resting when you need to — this is not a race. Draw a few houses a day and you'll have a thriving, bustling town on your wall in no time.

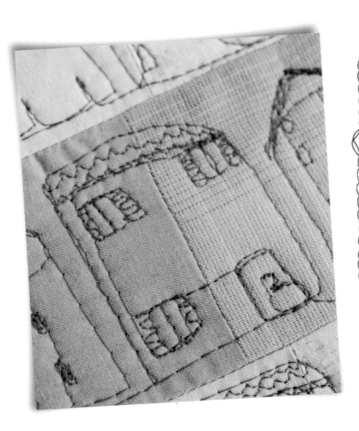

Requirements

Pale strips of fabric for background between 1½in–2½in (3.8cm–6.4cm) wide and 3½in–4½in (9cm–11.4cm) long
Wadding (batting) 10½in (26.7cm) square
Deep grey polyester thread
Wooden frame 10½in (26.7cm) square
Staple gun and staples

Finished size: 10½in (26.7cm) square

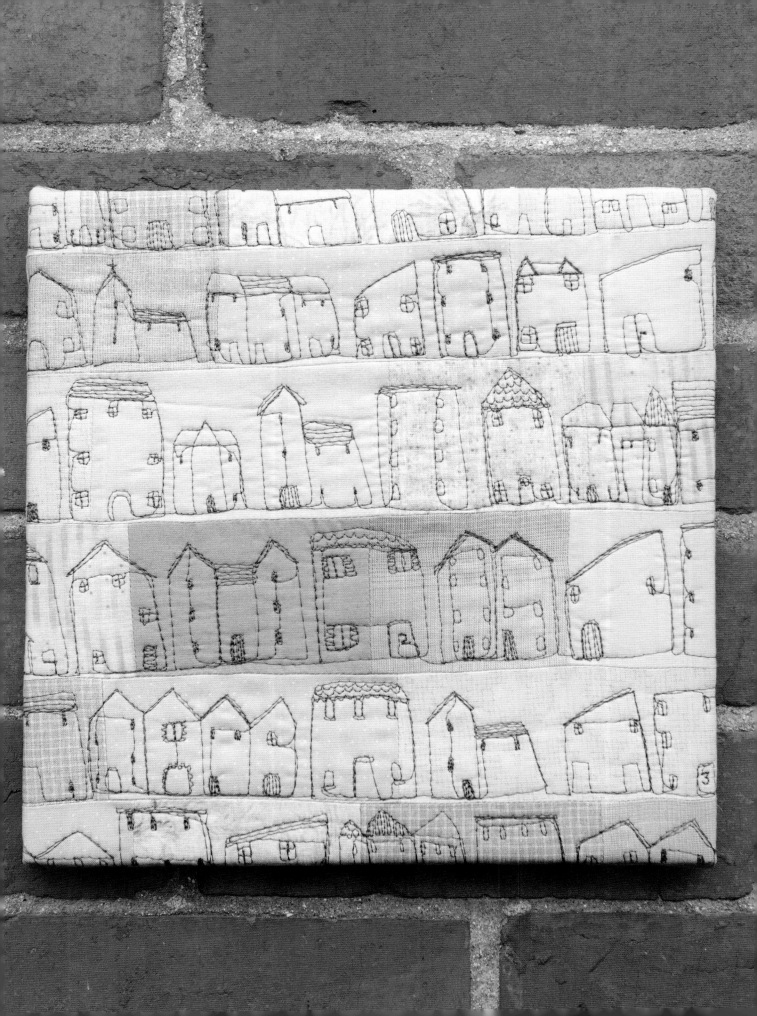

INSTRUCTIONS

1 **Prepare the background fabric:** Cut the pale fabric strips 1½in–2½in (3.8cm–6.4cm) wide and 3½in–4½in (9cm x 11.4cm) long. Chain piece these together until you have a pieced cloth that measures about 10½in (26.7cm) square. Press and trim to size if necessary.

2 **Free-motion quilt:** Place the wadding (batting) behind the background fabric. Set your machine to free-motion quilting (put the feed dogs down and add your special darning foot) and sewing with deep grey thread stitch the houses in rows. Start from the top left of the fabric and work each row separately, drawing the houses with a continuous line of stitches. Outline the shapes of the houses and add windows and other details as you go. Take regular breaks. For more guidance see Techniques: Free-Motion Quilting. When you've finished, pull threads to the reverse of the fabric and tie off securely.

3 **Make the wooden frame:** This is quite straight forward, just cut your wood to size and then nail or staple the pieces securely in place at the corners. Ensure that the edges are flush and smooth and that they form right angles. The frame will not be seen so don't worry too much!

4 **Finish and frame:** The finished stitching is mounted over the frame, with the edges tucked over to the back and stapled in place. See details of how to do this in Techniques: Making a Wooden Frame.

DETACHED HOUSES

I've wanted to make some little houses for a long time, and finally I have! I'm really pleased with these detached houses all standing in a row. I made all three of these in one evening — they are a little bit fiddly but don't take long to make. I tried sewing them together on the machine but I didn't like how they turned out, so please take the time to hand stitch them — they will look better and you'll be happier.

The houses are filled with rice so have a very pleasing weight to them. In fact, three might not be enough — keep stitching until you have a whole street! They would also make wonderful pincushions to give as gifts.

Requirements for one house

Blanket, felt or similar non-fraying fabric 9in (23cm) square

Uncooked rice or sand

Cream sewing thread and grey embroidery thread

Finished size: 2in x 3in (5cm x 7.6cm)

Template needed: house layout template

INSTRUCTIONS

1 Make the paper template: Photocopy or trace the template from the Template section onto paper. Carefully cut out on the outside lines.

2 Prepare fabric: Press your fabric if necessary and then place the template on top of the fabric and cut out the house shape.

3 Embroider: Decide which will be the front of your house and using small stitches and grey embroidery silk, embroider as many windows and doors as you wish (Fig 1).

4 Hand stitch: Fold up the house so that the walls and the roof touch. Take your time and carefully sew one pair of walls together using a whip stitch and small stitches. Keep your stitches neat as this is the right side of the house and they will be seen. Keep sewing the house together leaving a 1in (2.5cm) opening in the roof for the filling.

5 Fill and finish: Fill the house with rice (or sand if using as a pincushion). Using whip stitch and small stitches carefully stitch the roof opening closed (Fig 2). Your little house is made!

Fig 1

Fig 2

Little Idea...

Key Ring

Every key needs a lovely key
ring – why don't you draw
a picture of your house on
yours and embroidery it with
free-machine stitching?

TERRACED HOUSES CUSHION

I wanted to make a cushion with simple patchwork houses on and here it is — and the town chapter seems just the right home for it. The piecing is simple and quick to do and the windows and doors add just enough detail to make it interesting. Of course, you could add embroidery or beads to your cushion. Or why not have brightly coloured windows and doors?

There's also no reason why you couldn't make a quilt from this design — just keep stitching and stitching and there it will be!

Requirements

Fabric for houses, twelve rectangles each 3½in x 3in (9cm x 7.6cm)

Fabric for roofs, twelve rectangles each 3½in x 2in (9cm x 5cm)

Scraps of fabrics for appliqué

Small piece of fusible web

Fabric for cushion's envelope backs, two rectangles 12½in x 9in (31.8cm x 23cm)

Grey sewing thread

Cushion pad to fit

Finished size: 12in (30.5cm) square

INSTRUCTIONS

1 Prepare fabrics: Wash and press all your fabric before starting. Cut all the terraced houses fabrics to the sizes noted in the Requirements list, ready to piece them together.

2 Chain piece: Piece your rectangles together to make three rows of houses and three rows of roofs. Press the pieces. Sew the roof rows onto the house rows, matching the seams as well as you can until you have made the cushion front.

3 Prepare the appliqué: Prepare door and window appliques for your terraced houses following the instructions in Techniques: Fusible Web Appliqué. My windows were about ⅜in (1cm) square and the doors were about ⅜in–¾in (1cm–2cm). Arrange all your appliqué pieces very carefully as once the appliqué is pressed in place with the iron it cannot be removed.

4 Stitch the appliqué: Set your sewing machine up for free-motion quilting and using grey thread, stitch around the terraced houses, windows and doors. I added roof tiles and shingles to the roofs for added texture and interest. You can add as much detail as you like – just have confidence! For more guidance see Techniques: Free-Motion Quilting.

5 Make the cushion envelope backs: Cut two 12½in x 9in (31.8cm x 23cm) rectangles. Fold ½in (1.3cm) up along one long side to form a hem. Press, fold over again and press. Stitch in place. Repeat this process for the other rectangle.

6 Pin the cushion: Place the cushion front on a table, right side up. Place one of the envelope backs on top of the cushion front, aligning the edges at the top and with right sides together. Pin in place (Fig 1). Place the second envelope back on top, aligning the bottom edges and with right sides together. Pin in place (Fig 2). You will only be able to see the wrong side of your cushion backs now.

Fig 1

Fig 2

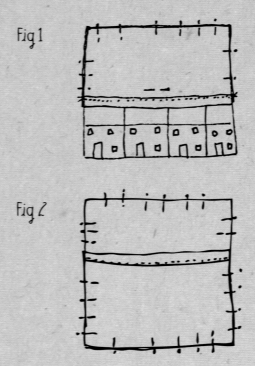

7 Finish the cushion: Starting on the right-hand side of your cushion, 3in (7.6cm) away from the corner, sew all the way round your cushion, pivoting at a right angle at the corners to keep your corners sharp. When you are back to where you started, secure your stitches and cut the excess fabric away from the corners, cutting close to your stitches but not through them (Fig 3). Turn the cushion the right way out and insert your cushion pad. All finished!

Fig 3

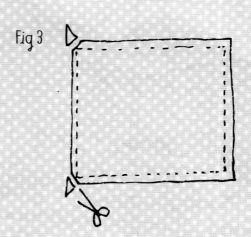

Little Idea...

Embroidered Tea Towel

Adding some simple free-machine embroidery to a pretty lace tea towel might make the drying up a little more interesting!

COUNTRY

VILLAGE SQUARES QUILT

We have good friends who live deep in the country and it's always a treat to visit them and get away from all the hustle and bustle of town. I enjoy walking through the quiet lanes, admiring the charming old cottages and imagining how life would be if I lived there. I'd definitely keep chickens!

This quilt was inspired by my many country walks and imaginings and is perfect for a single bed. I took great pleasure in drawing all the cottages, barns and little houses. You have twelve squares to appliqué however you wish — I wonder how many chickens and windmills your quilt will have?

Requirements

Fabric for twelve appliqué blocks 2yd/m

Selection of mixed fabrics for appliqué motifs (about 6in/15.2cm squares)

Fabric for sashing and border 2yd/m

Backing fabric 3yd (2.75m)

Binding fabric ½yd/m

Wadding (batting) 50in x 65in (127cm x 165cm)

Fusible web 1yd/m

Polyester sewing threads: neutral for piecing and dark grey for free-machining

Water-soluble fabric pen

Machine quilting thread

Finished size: 48in x 63in (122cm x 160cm)

Templates needed: various cottages, thatched cottage, row of cottages, barn, windmill, cat, birds, tree, bush, fence, chickens and sheep. The tractor, trailer, fork and spade are used in the Village Map Quilt

Fig 1

Border strips 3½in x 57½in
(8.9cm x 146cm)

Appliqué blocks 12½in
(32cm) square

Sashing strips 3½in x 42½in
(8.9cm x 108cm)

Sashing rectangles
3½in x 12½in (9cm x 32cm)

Border strips 3½in x 48½in
(8.9cm x 123.2cm)

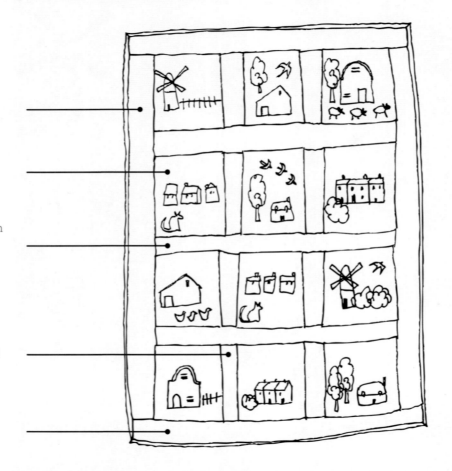

6 Sew sashing to blocks: Fig 1 shows the quilt layout of three appliqué blocks each in four rows. Take your first appliqué block and using a ¼in (6mm) seam allowance sew a 3½in x 12½in (8.9cm x 32cm) sashing rectangle to the right-hand side, as shown in Fig 2. Now sew the left-hand side of your second appliqué block to the sashing and so on. Continue in this way until you have made four separate rows of three appliqué blocks. Press the seams.

Fig 2

7 Sew rows together: With right sides together and using a ¼in (6mm) seam allowance, stitch a plain sashing strip to the bottom of your first appliqué row. Press and then sew the top of the second appliqué row to the bottom of the plain sashing. Pin carefully to ensure the appliqué blocks in each row will align. Continue in this way until you have sewn all four appliqué rows and three plain sashing rows together.

8 Sew border: Sew the long border strips to the left and right sides of the quilt. Sew the remaining strips across the top and bottom to complete the quilt top. Press carefully.

9 Prepare to quilt: I prefer to mark up my quilting lines *before* I make the quilt sandwich. Choose your quilting method (I hand quilted) and mark up with your chosen design. Using a water-soluble fabric pen I drew around a dinner plate for the large circles and a glass for the smaller circles. Cut the backing fabric bigger than required, approximately 50in x 65in (127cm x 165cm) – depending on the width of your fabric you may need to piece the fabric first. Using the backing fabric and wadding (batting), prepare the quilt sandwich as described in Techniques: Making a Quilt Sandwich.

10 Quilt: Hand quilt in small, even running stitches beginning at the centre of the quilt and working out gradually in all directions to ensure the layers sit smoothly. For further guidance on quilting see Techniques: Quilting. When you have finished, remove any visible quilting lines. Check your quilt is straight and the right size, trimming if necessary.

43

11 Bind the quilt: Prepare sufficient binding to go around your quilt, plus 8in (20cm). If necessary, refer to Techniques: Binding. Now sew the binding in place all around your quilt – see Techniques: Stitching the Binding for details.

12 Finish off: All quilts deserve a label, which should include your name and the date the quilt was finished. You could embroider directly onto the quilt or make a little patch of fabric to slipstitch in place – see Techniques: Labelling a Quilt. Time to show your quilt off to everyone!

Little Idea...

Thatched Cottage Brooch:

A free-machine drawing of a little cottage is easily made into a brooch by stitching a safety pin to the back.

VILLAGE MAP QUILT

When I was little one of my favourite books was *Milly Molly Mandy*. On the endpapers of the book was a line–drawn map of the village her family lived in. It used to fascinate me and now (after rather a long time) the map has inspired me to design this village quilt with its cottages and their connecting lanes.

This quilt has a wholecloth background, so you can put cottages, barns and sheep wherever you like. Add trees, birds and chickens and there it is — your country village. Then, pick up your needle and meander through the land with your quilting stitches, pausing at cottages and windmills to admire the view.

Requirements

Fabric for wholecloth background 1½yd/m

Selection of mixed fabrics for appliqué motifs (about 6in/15.2cm squares)

Backing fabric 1½yd/m

Binding fabric ½yd/m

Wadding (batting) 40in x 59in (102cm x 150cm)

Fusible web 1yd/m

Water-soluble fabric pen

Dark grey polyester thread for free-motion stitching

Hand quilting thread

Brown wool or thick cotton thread

Finished size: 36in x 54in (91.5cm x 137cm)

Templates needed: use the same templates as the Village Squares Quilt

INSTRUCTIONS

1 Prepare fabrics: Wash and press all fabrics before you start. Trim the wholecloth fabric background to size after careful pressing. Alternatively, you could leave the background a little larger and trim it down later after all the appliqué is complete.

2 Prepare the appliqués: Use the templates provided and your selection of mixed fabrics to prepare the appliqués following the instructions in Techniques: Fusible Web Appliqué. Arrange all appliqué pieces carefully on the background fabric as once they are pressed in place with the iron they cannot be removed. Fig 1 shows the layout I used.

Fig 1

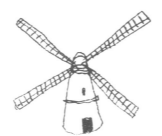

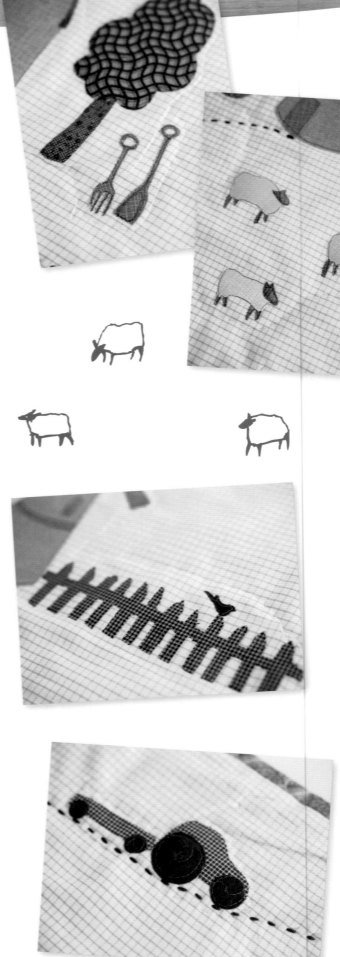

3 Stitch the appliqués: Set your sewing machine up for free-motion quilting and using a contrasting thread, stitch round the cottages and other motifs one at a time, adding as much detail as you dare! Try to be confident – go on, you can do it! For more guidance see Techniques: Free-Motion Quilting.

4 Prepare to quilt: I prefer to mark up my quilting lines before I make the quilt sandwich. Using a water-soluble fabric pen draw a wandering line around the cottages and trees to make a path all around the village (Fig 1). Cut the backing fabric and wadding (batting) bigger than required, approximately 40in x 59in (102cm x 150cm). Using the backing fabric, wadding and quilt top, prepare the quilt sandwich as described in Techniques: Making a Quilt Sandwich.

5 Quilt: Hand quilt around the motifs in small, even running stitches beginning at the centre of the quilt and working out gradually in all directions to ensure the layers sit smoothly. Hand quilt the paths in larger running stitches and a thicker thread (such as brown wool). For further guidance on quilting see Techniques: Quilting. When you have finished, remove any visible quilting lines. Check the quilt is straight and the right size, trimming if necessary.

6 Bind the quilt: Prepare sufficient binding to go around your quilt, plus about 8in (20cm). If necessary, refer to Techniques: Binding. Now sew the binding in place all around your quilt – see Techniques: Stitching the Binding.

7 Finish off: All quilts deserve a label, which should include your name and the date the quilt was finished. You could embroider directly onto the quilt or make a little patch of fabric to slipstitch in place – see Techniques: Labelling a Quilt. Now show your quilt off to everyone!

WOODLAND COTTAGE HANGING

I've always loved vintage needlework samplers and maybe one day I'll find one in a thrift shop for a price I can afford. Alternatively, I could embroider one and hope my family keep it for a hundred years! But until then I can be inspired by their naïve charm. So, here is my quick appliqué version of a charming house needlework sampler I once saw. Feel free to add the alphabet and other little motifs to yours — or an improving text to be traditional!

Requirements

Background fabric 23in x 12in (58.5cm x 30.5cm)

Scraps of brown and grey fabric for cottage appliqué

Scraps of green and brown for trees and shrubs, pale grey for birds appliqué

Wadding (batting) 23in x 12in (58.5cm x 30.5cm)

Fusible web for appliqué

Pale beige quilting thread

Deep grey polyester sewing thread

Removable fabric marking pen

Wooden frame 19in x 8in (48.5cm x 20.5cm)

Staple gun and staples

Finished size: 19in x 8in (48.5cm x 20.5cm)

Templates needed: thatched cottage, tree, shrub and birds for appliqué (as used in the Village Squares Quilt) and the long feather wave quilting template (as used in the Windy Day Picture)

INSTRUCTIONS

1 Prepare fabrics and wadding: Press all your fabrics. Cut the appliqué background fabric and wadding (batting) to the correct size.

2 Work the appliqué: Use the templates provided in the Templates section and your appliqué fabrics to prepare the appliqués for the cottage, trees, shrubs and birds, following the instructions in Techniques: Fusible Web Appliqué. First arrange the cottage in the centre of the fabric and then add the other motifs. Remember to leave a minimum of 2in (5cm) clear all around the appliqué to allow for the fabric to be folded and stapled to the frame later. Press carefully to fuse the appliqués into place.

3 Mark up quilting: Use the template provided and a removable fabric pen or pencil and trace one long wave quilting template onto the background fabric. The design is drawn behind the cottage and trees and will add texture and interest when quilted later.

4 Free-motion quilt: Place the wadding (batting) behind the appliqué background fabric. Set your machine to free-motion quilting (put the feed dogs down and add your special darning foot) and working with the deep grey or brown thread quilt the cottage, outlining the shape and adding windows and other details as you go. Do the same for the trees, shrubs and birds. Pull threads to the reverse of the fabric and tie off securely. For more guidance see Techniques: Free-Motion Quilting.

5 Hand quilt: With small, even running stitches hand quilt the feather wave using pale beige quilting thread. For more guidance on quilting see Techniques: Hand Quilting. Remove any remaining pen lines.

6 Make the wooden frame: To be honest, I asked my husband to do this for me! It is quite straight forward though, just cut your wood to size and then nail or staple the pieces securely in place at the corners. Ensure that the edges are flush and smooth and that they form right angles. The frame will not be seen, so don't worry too much!

7 Finish and frame: The finished stitching is mounted over the frame, with the edges tucked over to the back and stapled in place. See details of how to do this in Techniques: Making a Wooden Frame.

Little Idea...

EMBROIDERED WINDMILL CUSHION

You can use any of the appliqué templates in the book for embroidery too, and a little cushion like this is a lovely way to show off your stitching.

ISOLATED COTTAGE PICTURE

Now, I'm certain I couldn't live happily for long in this tiny little cottage all alone in such a large landscape. But I must say, a week or two of utter quiet and isolation does have a certain appeal (particularly when my boys are squabbling!).

The success of this simple project lies in the careful and thoughtful combination of muted colours and the texture added by the hand quilting. I used Oakshott cottons (see Suppliers).

Requirements

Fabrics in muted colours, to cut rectangles maximum size 2in x 4in (5cm x 10.2cm)

Backing fabric 17½in x 10½in (44.4cm x 26.7cm)

Wadding (batting) 17½in x 10½in (44.4cm x 26.7cm)

Scraps of brown and grey fabrics for cottage appliqué

Fusible web for appliqué

Pale grey or beige quilting thread

Deep grey polyester sewing thread

Removable fabric marking pen

Picture frame 22in x 19in (56cm x 48cm)

Beige mount board cut to fit frame, maximum 22in x 19in (56cm x 48cm)

Glue line or glue dots

Finished size: 17in x 10in (43cm x 25.5cm)

Templates needed: tiny cottage and circular feather wreath quilting template

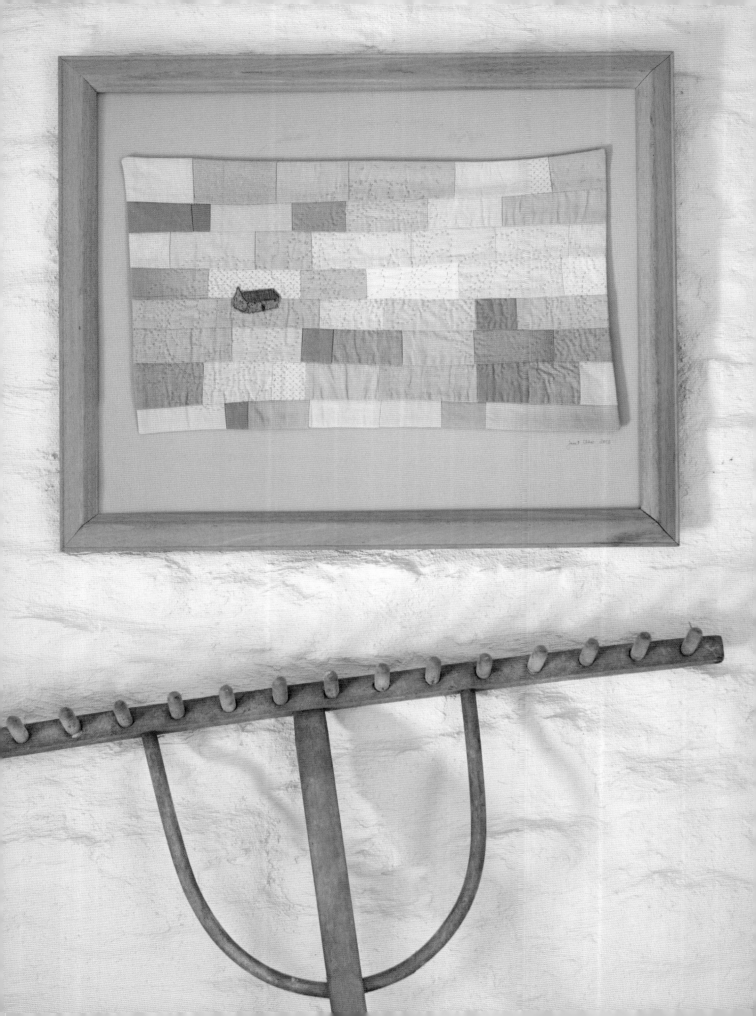

INSTRUCTIONS

1 Prepare fabrics: Press all your fabrics. I really didn't want this picture to be all straight lines, so I cut all the fabric by eye with scissors. If this worries you, please cut as usual with a rotary cutter. For the appliqué background you need to cut rectangles of different sizes, between 1½in x 1in (3.8cm x 2.5cm) and 2in x 4in (5cm x 10.2cm). Cut the backing fabric and wadding (batting) to the correct size.

2 Sew pieces together: Arrange your fabric into piles by width, but don't worry about sorting the colours. Chain piece these together on the sewing machine, stitching pairs of same-width rectangles right sides together (Fig 1). Snip the threads between the fabric pairs and then repeat, so that you are sewing the pairs into fours and so on. Repeat this until you have lengths of fabric measuring 18in (46cm) and then press.

3 Stitch appliqué background: Stitch the lengths of fabric together to form the background and press.

4 Prepare the appliqué: Use the template provided and your appliqué fabrics to prepare the little cottage appliqué following the instructions in Techniques: Fusible Web Appliqué. Arrange the cottage about 3½in (8.9cm) in from the left side of the fabric and 4½in (11.4cm) down from the top. Press carefully to fuse into place.

5 Mark up quilting: Using the template provided and a removable fabric pen or pencil, trace three feather wreath quilting templates onto the background fabric. You want the quilting to surround the cottage and add movement and texture to the landscape.

6 Free-motion quilt: Place the wadding (batting) behind the appliqué background fabric. Set your machine to free-motion quilting (put the feed dogs down and add your special darning foot) and working with the pale grey or beige thread quilt the cottage, outlining the shape and adding windows and other details as you go. Pull threads to the reverse of the fabric and tie off securely. For more guidance see Techniques: Free-Motion Quilting.

Fig 1

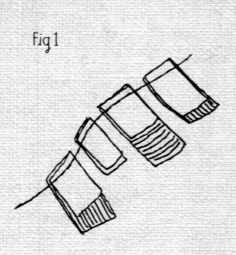

7 Hand quilt: With small, even running stitches hand quilt the feather wreaths (Fig 2). For more guidance on quilting see Techniques: Hand Quilting.

8 Add backing fabric: Place your appliqué picture right side up on a table. Place your backing fabric right side down on top of the appliqué. Pin together and start sewing 1in (2.5cm) away from the centre of one side with a ¼in (6mm) seam allowance. Continue, stopping ¼in (6mm) away from each corner, leave the needle in the fabric and lift the presser foot to swivel the fabric and continue stitching the next side. Repeat for all four corners. Stop stitching 2in–3in (5cm–7.6cm) away from where you began. You should have all the corners neatly sewn and an opening to turn the picture the right way out. Trim the excess fabric away from the corners. Turn right side out, teasing the corners gently to get them as sharp as you can. Fold both the seam allowances at the opening inside the picture and then slipstitch the opening closed. Press the edges very lightly, taking care not to flatten the texture you so carefully hand quilted in.

9 Finish and frame: Check your appliqué picture for pieces of lint and stray threads before mounting in the frame. You can easily remove any you find by dabbing the surface lightly with a piece of sticky tape. Cut your mount board to the exact size of your picture frame. Attach a glue line or glue dots to the reverse top edge of the appliqué picture. Position the picture on the mount board and press the glue line firmly in place. Do not position the picture in the centre of the mount board – there should be a slightly larger piece of board showing at the bottom than at the top. Sign and date your picture and show it off to everyone.

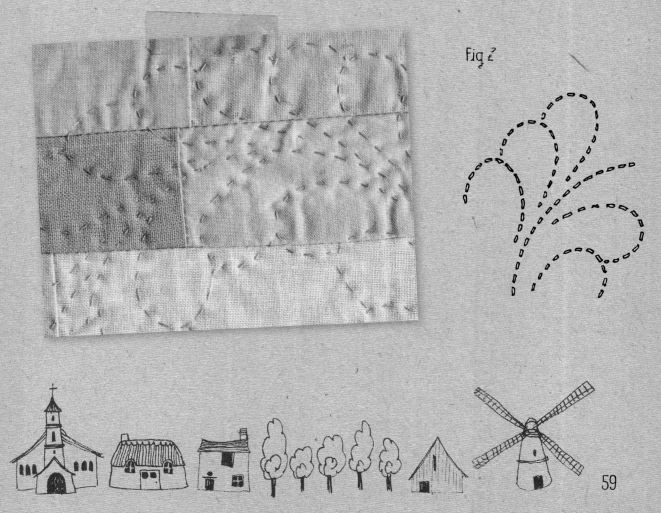

Fig 2

COUNTRY LANE TABLE RUNNER

I was going to appliqué a ready-made white linen table runner but fell in love with this dove grey wool fabric and just had to use it instead.

Remember to turn some of your cottages and little houses upside down so everyone at the table has a pretty country property to admire. There is no reason why you couldn't make town and coastal table runners as well. My finished runner measured 14in x 56in (35.5cm x 142cm) but you could alter your measurements to fit your table.

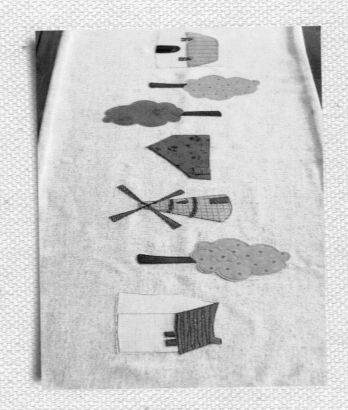

Requirements

Wool tweed fabric 1¾yd/m or 1yd/m if you don't mind a seam in the centre of the runner

Selection of cotton fabrics in browns and greens for appliqué

Fusible web 1yd/m

Deep grey polyester sewing thread

Finished size: 14in x 56in (35.5cm x 142cm)

Templates needed: six buildings, a tree and a windmill

Fig 1A

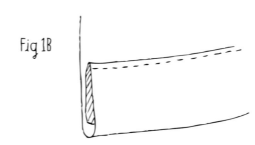

Fig 1B

Fig 2

5 Free-motion quilt: Set your sewing machine up for free-motion quilting (put the feed dogs down and add your special darning foot) and, using a dark grey thread, start stitching the most central image, outlining the shape and adding windows and other details as you go. Be brave and add life to your appliqué! Continue like this with the rest of the appliqués. For more guidance see Techniques: Free-Motion Quilting.

6 Finish off: Pull threads to the reverse of the fabric and tie off securely. Place the runner on your table and gather everyone in the house together to admire it. Tell them that the first person to spill something on your beautiful runner has to do the washing up!

Little Idea...

Glass Jar Drawing

Why not buy a porcelain pen from an art shop and upcycle a simple glass jar with a sweet little cottage drawing?

COAST

SEA AND SHORE QUILT

I wanted to make a seaside quilt with a bold patchwork centre surrounded by the shore and its houses. I chose a Log Cabin patchwork block design and kept the traditional red central squares that represent the heart and hearth of the home. You can imagine all the weary sailors glad to see the welcoming lights on the shore.

I created all sorts of coastal houses for this quilt. There are lighthouses to get sailors safely home, house boats and boat houses, beach huts and cottages of all shapes and sizes — just like the real coast. I imagined cuddling up with this quilt and a nice cup of tea whilst gazing out to sea watching the moonlight on the water. And one day I will do just that, but until then my quilt will keep me warm on the sofa, in my town house!

Requirements

Fabrics for Log Cabin centre: four 2½in (6.5cm) squares and forty-eight strips in total, maximum size 1½in x 9in (4cm x 23cm)

Fabric for appliqué background 1½yd/m

Selection of mixed fabrics for appliqué, maximum 7in x 4in (18cm x 10.5cm)

Yellow border fabric ½yd/m

Red border fabric ½yd/m

Backing fabric 1½yd/m

Binding fabric ½yd/m

Wadding (batting) 49in (125cm) square

Fusible web 1yd/m

Polyester sewing thread: dark grey for free-motion stitching and cream thread for machine quilting

Finished size: 45½in (115.6cm) square approx

Templates needed: boat, beach hut, lighthouse, flag, birds, fish, cottage, plus other cottages of your choice from the Village Squares Quilt templates

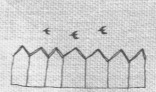

INSTRUCTIONS

1 Prepare fabrics: Wash and press all your fabrics before you start. Cut the central squares and the strips for the Log Cabin centre blocks.

2 Make a Log Cabin block: Take a red centre square and the palest fabric strip, place raw edges and right sides together and stitch along one side. Press and trim away the excess fabric strip. Take your second pale strip and sew that to the first strip and the red central square. Press and trim as before. The next two strips are blue and are added in the same way (Fig 1).

Continue until you have stitched six pale strips and six blue strips round each red square (Fig 2 and Fig 3). Press the finished block – it should measure 8½in (21.6cm) square. Make four more blocks like this.

3 Make the quilt centre: Arrange the four Log Cabin blocks in a pleasing colour arrangement – I chose to place the pale colours together in the centre. Stitch the blocks together and press seams. The centre should now measure 16½in (42cm) square including seam allowance.

Fig 1

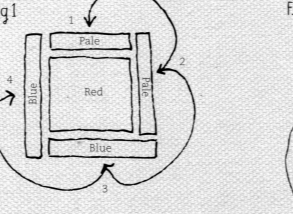
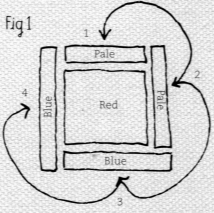

Fig 2

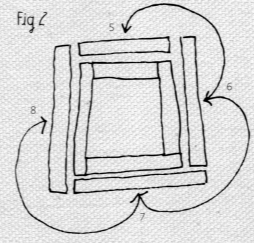

Fig 3

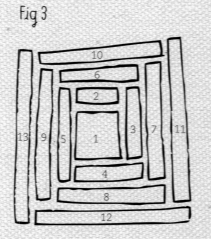

4 Cut the border fabrics: For the appliqué background border, cut the fabric into two pieces 12½in x 16½in (31.8cm x 42cm) and two pieces 12½in x 40½in (31.8cm x 103cm).

For the yellow border, cut two strips 2½in x 40½in (6.3cm x 102.9cm) and two strips 2½in x 44½in (6.3cm x 113cm).

For the red border, cut two strips 1¼in x 44½in (3.2cm x 113cm) and two strips 1¼in x 46in (3.2cm x 116.8cm).

5 Sew on the appliqué border: Sew the shorter border strips to the top and bottom of the Log Cabin quilt centre. Press seams and trim. Sew the longer strips to the left side and right side of the quilt centre. Press and trim. Sewing the appliqué border fabric in place now makes arranging the motifs easier.

6 Prepare the appliqués: Use a selection of templates and your mixed fabrics to prepare the beach huts and other motifs following the instructions in Techniques: Fusible Web Appliqué. Arrange all your appliqué pieces very carefully on the background fabric as once they are pressed in place with the iron they cannot be removed.

7 Stitch the appliqués: Set your sewing machine up for free-motion quilting and using the dark grey thread, stitch around the outline of the motifs. You can add more details to the appliqué motifs, such as windows, doors, names or numbers. For more guidance see Techniques: Free-Motion Quilting.

8 Stitch the borders: Stitch the yellow borders to the quilt, starting with the shorter top and bottom pieces. Press and trim. Now stitch on the left and right borders. Press and trim to size. Repeat this process to add the red outer border.

9 Prepare to quilt: Cut the backing fabric and wadding (batting) bigger than required, approximately 49in (124.5cm) square. Using the backing fabric, wadding and quilt top, prepare the quilt sandwich as described in Techniques: Making a Quilt Sandwich.

10 Machine quilt: Set your machine to sew with a medium size stitch and, starting from the very centre, stitch out towards the corners in a diagonal line. Repeat until the whole quilt has been diagonally quilted in both directions. My quilting lines are 1½in (3.8cm) apart. I attached a quilting guide bar to my sewing machine and used that to guide my quilting instead of marking up the quilt top (Fig 4).

11 Bind the quilt: Prepare sufficient 3in (7.6cm) wide binding to go around your quilt, plus 8in (20cm). If necessary, refer to Techniques: Binding. Now sew the binding in place all around your quilt – see Techniques: Stitching the Binding.

12 Finish off: All quilts deserve a label, which should include your name and the date the quilt was finished. You could embroider directly onto the quilt or make a little patch of fabric to slipstitch in place – see Techniques: Labelling a Quilt. Now show your quilt off to everyone.

Fig 4

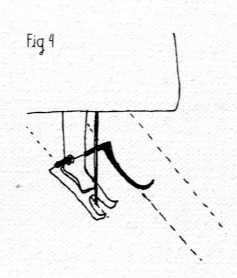

BEACH HUTS AND GULLS QUILT

I was thinking about the sort of quilt I'd like to have with me on a summery day at the coast and decided it would need to be simple and refreshingly coloured, big enough to lie on for a picnic and to wrap myself in when the inevitable chill set in, but small enough to carry (the car is rarely able to be left near the spot you actually want to sit in in my experience). I felt it also needed to be quick to make and easily washable, so it could really live life to the full. So, enjoy making your quilt but please enjoy using it more!

I made a scrappy binding for the quilt, using 3in (7.6cm) wide strips of the assorted fabrics I used for the beach hut appliqués, but you could use a single colour if you prefer.

Requirements

Wholecloth background 1¼yd/m

Selection of mixed fabrics for beach huts appliqué – maximum 6in x 4in (15.2cm x 10.2cm)

White fabric for gulls' appliqué

Backing fabric 1¼yd/m

Binding made from short strips of assorted fabrics or ½yd/m if using a single fabric

Wadding (batting) 46in (117cm) square

Fusible web 1yd/m

Polyester sewing thread in white, red and blue for free-machine stitching and machine tying

Finished size: 42in (107cm) square

Templates needed: beach hut and gull (as used in the Sea and Shore Quilt and the Beach Hut Cushion)

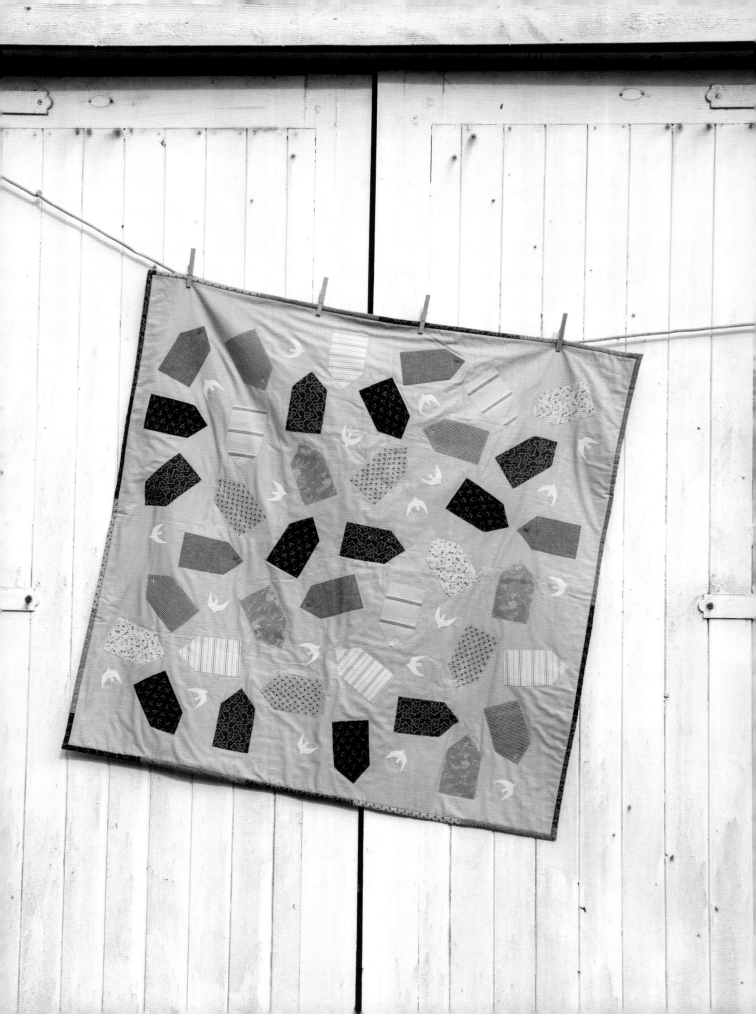

INSTRUCTIONS

1 Prepare fabrics: Wash and press all your fabrics before you start. Trim the wholecloth fabric background to size after careful pressing.

2 Prepare the appliqués: Use the templates provided and your selection of mixed fabrics to prepare the beach huts and gulls appliqués following the instructions in Techniques: Fusible Web Appliqué. I made thirty-nine huts and twenty gulls. Arrange all your appliqué pieces carefully on the background fabric as once they are pressed in place with the iron they cannot be removed. I kept rotating the fabric and placing huts in every direction and angle, and then added gulls in the gaps.

3 Stitch the appliqués: Set your sewing machine up for free-motion quilting and using a matching thread, stitch round the outline of the huts and gulls one at a time. I didn't add any stitching details to the appliqué motifs, but you could if you want to. For more guidance see Techniques: Free-Motion Quilting.

4 Prepare to quilt: Cut the backing fabric and the wadding (batting) bigger than required, approximately 46in (117cm) square. Using the backing fabric, wadding and quilt top, prepare the quilt sandwich as described in Techniques: Making a Quilt Sandwich.

5 Machine tie: I wanted this quilt to be soft and loose, so decided to tie the three layers together on the sewing machine using one of its embroidery stitches – I used a cross (Fig 1). If your machine does not have this capability you could always hand embroider a cross, or tie the quilt by hand. Check your quilt is straight and the right size, trimming if necessary.

Fig 1

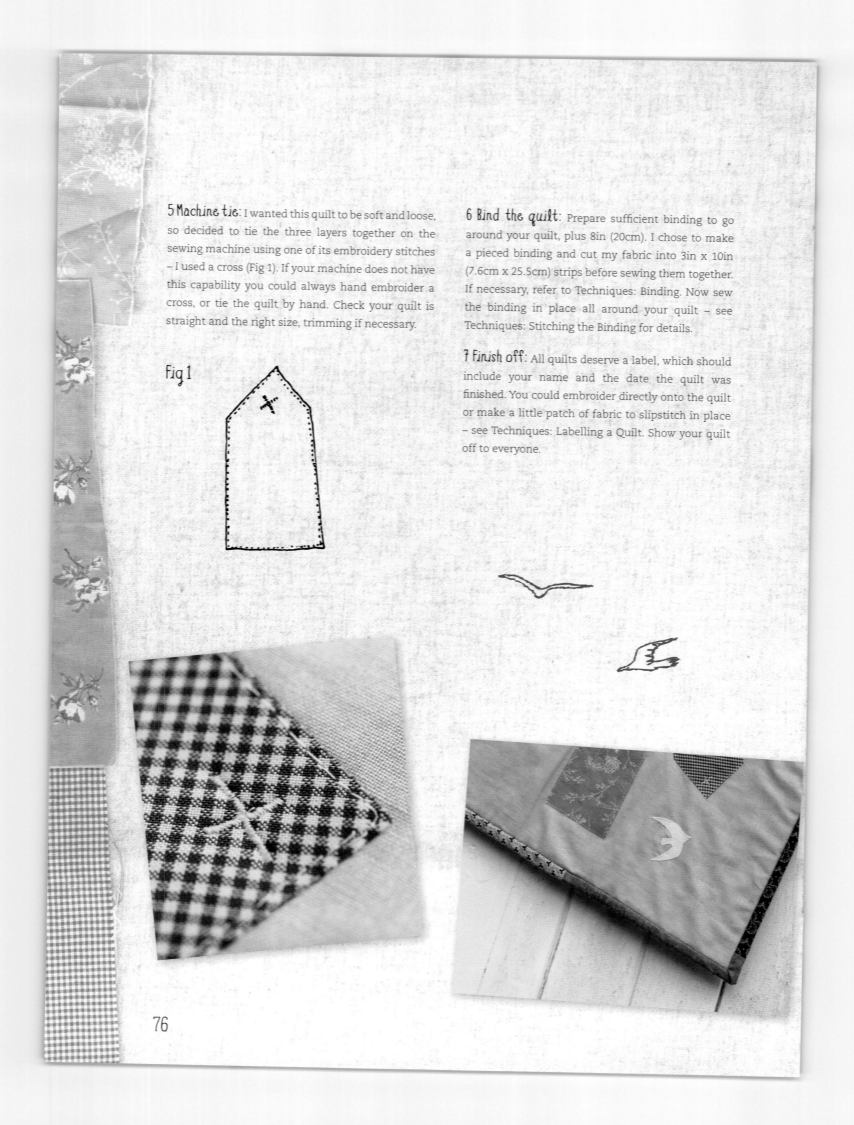

6 Bind the quilt: Prepare sufficient binding to go around your quilt, plus 8in (20cm). I chose to make a pieced binding and cut my fabric into 3in x 10in (7.6cm x 25.5cm) strips before sewing them together. If necessary, refer to Techniques: Binding. Now sew the binding in place all around your quilt – see Techniques: Stitching the Binding for details.

7 Finish off: All quilts deserve a label, which should include your name and the date the quilt was finished. You could embroider directly onto the quilt or make a little patch of fabric to slipstitch in place – see Techniques: Labelling a Quilt. Show your quilt off to everyone.

76

COASTAL COTTAGES WALL HANGING

This little wall hanging practically made itself! The cottages and beach huts just fell into place and the hand quilting was a pleasant evening's work. I just loved the rich blue colour of the background fabric and was reminded of twilight walks along the promenade, with the sky darkening and the cottages glowing slightly in the gloom.

Requirements

Background fabric 19in x 9in
(48.3cm x 23cm)

Wadding (batting) 19in x 9in
(48.3cm x 23cm)

Scraps of pale, brown and grey fabrics for
cottages appliqué

Scraps of striped fabrics for the beach
huts appliqué

Fusible web

Blue quilting thread

Deep grey polyester sewing thread

Removable fabric marking pen

Wooden frame 15in x 5in
(38cm x 12.7cm)

Staple gun and staples

Finished size: 15in x 5in (38cm x 12.7cm)

Templates needed: two small cottages
and beach hut, plus the wave quilting
template

INSTRUCTIONS

1 Prepare fabrics and wadding: Press all your fabrics. Cut the appliqué background fabric and wadding (batting) to the correct size.

2 Work the appliqué: Use the templates provided and your appliqué fabrics to prepare the row of beach huts and cottages following the instructions in Techniques: Fusible Web Appliqué. Arrange them by eye so they form a slightly wobbly line in the centre of the fabric. Leave a minimum of 2in (5cm) clear all around the edges of the appliqué to allow for the fabric to be folded and stapled to the frame. Press carefully to fuse the appliqués into place.

3 Mark up quilting: Use the template provided and a removable fabric pen or pencil, trace one long wave quilting template onto the background fabric. The quilting needs to be behind the cottages and beach huts to add texture and interest.

4 Free-motion quilt: Place the wadding (batting) behind the background fabric. Set your machine to free-motion quilting (put the feed dogs down and add your special darning foot) and working with deep grey thread, quilt the cottages, outlining the shapes and adding tiny windows and doors as you go. Pull threads to the back of the fabric and tie off securely. For more guidance see Techniques: Free-Motion Quilting.

5 Hand quilt: With small, even running stitches hand quilt the wave using the blue quilting thread. For more guidance see Techniques: Hand Quilting. Remove any remaining marking pen lines.

6 Make the wooden frame: Cut your wood to size and then nail or staple the pieces securely in place at the corners. Ensure that the edges are flush and smooth and that they form right angles.

7 Finish and frame: The finished stitching is mounted over the frame, with the edges tucked over onto the back and stapled in place. For details of how to do this refer to Techniques: Making a Wooden Frame.

Little Idea...

BEACH CUSHION

Three beach hut appliqués fit perfectly on a cushion, with a single gull wheeling in the sky – easy to make but so lovely.

WINDY DAY PICTURE

I love to walk along the sea cliff paths out of season, when it is quiet. I pretend it is all mine, with the wind blowing and the waves and gulls bustling round me. This framed wall hanging depicts my ideal scene.

One day I will live in a little thatched cottage as close to the sea as I can be. I'll beachcomb every day and then sit all wrapped up in a quilt and stare out to sea with a cup of tea. But I'll happily leave living in a lighthouse to someone braver! In the meantime I shall have to keep saving my pennies and being content with my daydreams.

Requirements

Very pale blue cotton, two 9½in (24cm) squares for background and backing

Wadding (batting) 9in (23cm) square

Scraps of brown, grey and cream fabric for appliqués

Fusible web for appliqué

Removable fabric marking pen

Dark grey polyester sewing thread

Pale grey or beige quilting thread

White mount board 16in (41cm) square

Picture frame 16in (41cm) square

Glue line or glue dots

Finished size: 9in (23cm) square

Templates needed: lighthouse, cottage, boat and gulls, feather quilting template

INSTRUCTIONS

1 Prepare fabrics: Press the fabrics. Cut the appliqué background, the backing fabric and the wadding (batting) to size using a rotary cutter and ruler.

2 Prepare appliqués: Use the templates provided and your appliqué fabrics to prepare the appliqués following the instructions in Techniques: Fusible Web Appliqué. Arrange all your appliqué pieces very carefully on the background fabric as once they are ironed in place they cannot be removed.

3 Mark up quilting: With a removable fabric pen or pencil, trace the feather wave quilting template onto the background fabric. You want the quilting to sweep past the lighthouse and the sail boat to add movement and texture.

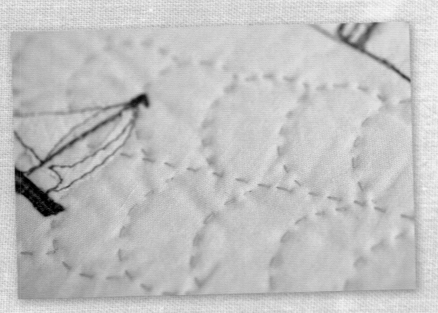

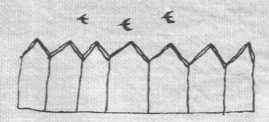

4 Add wadding: Place the wadding behind the appliqué background fabric.

5 Free-motion quilt: Set your machine to free-motion quilting (put the feed dogs down and add your special darning foot) and working with the dark grey thread, start stitching the most central image, outlining the shape and adding windows and other details as you go. Be brave and stitch life into your appliqué! Pull threads to the reverse of the fabric and tie off securely. For more guidance see Techniques: Free-Motion Quilting.

6 Quilt: Hand quilt the feather wave pattern with small, even running stitches. For more guidance see Techniques: Hand Quilting. After all that stitching your fabric is probably not square anymore, so check and then trim the edges a little to neaten them again.

7 Add backing fabric: Place your appliqué picture right side up on a table. Place your backing fabric right side down on top of the appliqué. Start sewing 1in (2.5cm) away from the centre of one side with a ¼in (6mm) seam allowance. Continue, stopping ¼in (6mm) away from each corner, leave the needle in the fabric and lift the presser foot to swivel the fabric and continue stitching the next side. Repeat for all four corners. Stop stitching 2in–3in (5cm–7.6cm) away from where you began. You should now have all the corners neatly sewn and an opening to turn the picture the right way out. Trim the excess fabric away from the corners (Fig 1). Turn right side out, teasing the corners gently to get them as sharp as you can. Fold both the seam allowances at the opening inside the picture and slipstitch the opening closed. Press the edges very lightly, taking care not to flatten the texture you so carefully hand quilted in.

Fig 1

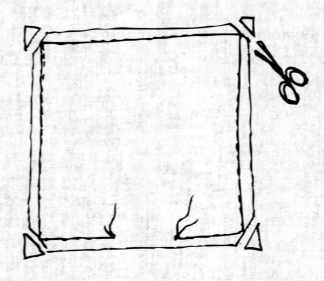

8 Finish and frame: Check your appliqué picture for pieces of lint and stray threads before mounting in the frame – you can easily remove any you find by dabbing the surface lightly with a piece of sticky tape. Cut your mount board to the exact size of your picture frame. Attach a glue line or glue dots to the reverse top edge of the appliqué picture. Position the picture on the mount board and press the glue line firmly in place. Do not position the picture in the centre of the mount board. There should be a slightly larger piece of mount board showing at the bottom than at the top. Once you have signed and dated your work you can show everyone your lovely picture.

Little Idea...

Free-Machined Napkins

Liven up a set of napkins with a free-machine stitched drawing of a lighthouse and sail boat.

BEACH HUT CUSHION

I've always been a tiny bit envious of the people you see at the seaside who have a beach hut to use. Whilst all our things are just scattered around on the sand being trodden on, the beach hut people have chairs, a little table and a pretty roof over their head for any sudden changes in the weather. Also, I rather fancy decorating a beach hut — wouldn't it be great fun?

My very own beach hut is a distant dream so I'll just have to make a beach hut—shaped cushion instead. I made this one in an evening so it's a quick and simple project. I've also drawn some embroidery decoration ideas for you should you wish to make a whole promenade of beach hut cushions.

Requirements

Wool blanket or similar, two 14in x 10in
(35.5cm x 25.5cm) rectangles
Cobalt blue wool embroidery thread
Cobalt blue stranded embroidery thread
Water-soluble fabric pen
Removable embroidery paper
Cushion filling (I bought a cheap cushion
and used the filling from that)

Finished size: 14in x 10in
(35.5cm x 25.5cm)

Templates needed: anchor, gull and
shingle roof tiles. Use the feather wave
quilting template from the Windy Day
Picture templates

INSTRUCTIONS

1 Prepare fabrics: Press your 14in x 10in (35.5cm x 25.4cm) rectangles of wool blanket.

2 Mark and cut fabric: Place the rectangles on a flat surface with the 10in (25.5cm) sides at the bottom. With an erasable fabric pen mark 4in (10.2cm) down from the top at the left and right edges, and then 4in (10.2cm) in from the bottom left corner. Measure 2½in (6.5cm) in from the left and right top corners. These marks will help you cut the roof off the cushion. Cut the top left and right triangular corners off between the marks you have made (Fig 1).

3 Draw the embroidery templates: Use the templates provided. The wool blanket is too thick to trace the templates through, so you will need to trace the templates onto a removable embroidery paper such as Stitch 'n' Tear and then embroider through that. Trace the shingle roof tiles, the anchor, the gull and the feather wave quilting template. Draw a vertical line between the two marks you made. Place the removable paper on top of the right side of one of the beach hut pieces of blanket.

4 Embroider: Using the cobalt blue wool embroidery thread and running stitch, embroider the shingle roof tiles and the vertical line. Using the same thread and backstitch, embroider the anchor and the outline of the gull. Remove the embroidery paper from these areas. Now fill in the gull using satin stitch. See Techniques: Embroidery for how to work these stitches.

5 Quilt: Divide the cobalt blue embroidery thread into three strands and with a neat running stitch hand quilt the feather wave (see Techniques: Hand Quilting). Carefully remove the remaining embroidery paper.

6 Sew together: Prepare your sewing machine. Pin the right sides of your beach hut pieces together. Using a ¼in (6mm) seam allowance, start sewing 1in (2.5cm) away from the bottom left-hand corner all around the cushion, pivoting at the corners. Continue stitching to within 3in (7.6cm) from where you started, leaving an opening at the bottom edge. Carefully trim away the excess fabric at the corners of your beach hut to remove bulk and allow the seams to lie neatly.

7 Finish off: Turn the cushion right side out. Stuff with cushion filling and then slipstitch the opening closed. Give your finished cushion a little hug! If you want to make more cushions, five further designs are shown as sketches here – or do your own thing!

Fig 1

2½in (6.3cm)

4in (10.2cm)

4in (10.2cm)

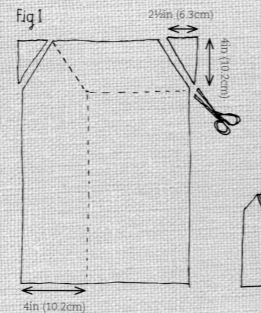

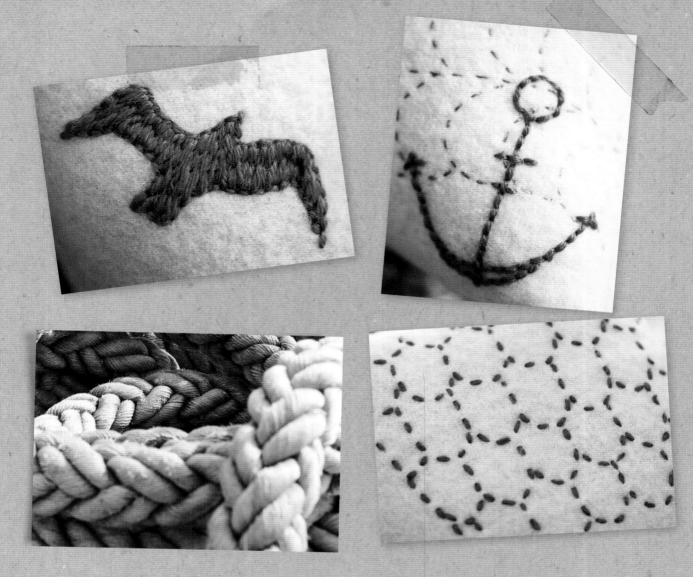

Little Idea...

Mug and Plate Drawings

It's easy to buy a porcelain pen from an art shop and then sketch little scenes to transform plain crockery.

TECHNIQUES

This section contains the information you will need to make the projects and finish them off beautifully. See Tools and Materials for advice on equipment you will need.

FABRIC

Washing fabric

It's important to wash and press all your fabric before using it in a quilt (Fig 1). Can you imagine how sad you'd be if the colours ran or the fabrics shrank when the finished quilt was washed for the first time?

Fig 1

Cutting fabric

Before cutting your fabric you should ensure that you are cutting it on the grain (Fig 2). This means cutting straight along one single thread in the weave. Fold your fabric with wrong sides together, aligning the selvedges and ignoring how un-even the tops of the fabric looks. Press your fabric as carefully and neatly as you can, keeping the selvedges together at all times. Place the selvedges on a vertical line on your cutting mat and with your rotary cutter trim the selvedges off, cutting through both layers of fabric at the same time. You can now assume that this cut edge is 'on the grain'. Touch it as little as possible and take all your subsequent measurements from it.

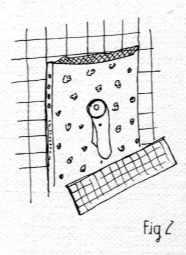

Fig 2

- When cutting fabric remember the old adage, 'measure twice and cut once'. Double check your measurements and when you are certain everything is as straight and accurate as can be, cut carefully with your rotary cutter.

Rotary cutter safety

Rotary cutters are blades on wheels and very, *very* sharp, so treat them with respect. Always cut away from yourself, place your hand on the ruler in an arched shape and keep your fingers well away from the edge (Fig 3). Get into the habit of always locking the blade away after every single cut and you'll be fine. A blunt rotary cutter is probably more dangerous than a sharp one, so keep replacing your cutter blades.

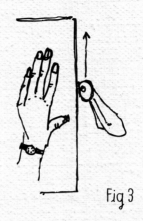

Fig 3

Seam allowance

Quilters use a very small seam allowance of a ¼in (0.635mm to be precise!) to reduce bulk at the seams and to be thrifty with their precious fabric. You can buy a quarter inch foot for your sewing machine, which helps with accurate piecing. The main point to remember is to be consistent – cut and sew with the same seam allowance and all will be well.

Pinning fabrics

When piecing fabrics together it's best to place your pins vertically in the fabric so they don't get caught under the machine foot (Fig 4). You can sew straight over them (and I often do) but it's probably best not to in case they get hit by the needle and snap.

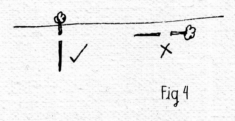

Fig 4

Chain piecing

This is the most efficient way to stitch lots of fabric pieces together, as it saves both time and thread. Pile your fabrics by the machine, pick up two and put the right sides of the fabric together and sew with a ¼in (6mm) seam allowance. When you reach the end of that pair of fabrics just continue sewing and feed the next pair through the machine (Fig 5). It will look like bunting! Cut the fabrics into pairs and then repeat the process again – sewing into fours, then eights and so on.

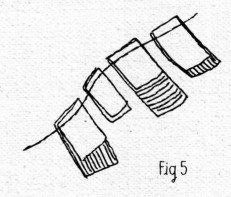

Fig 5

Pressing

Quilters *press* – they don't iron! Don't move the iron backwards and forwards over the seams: lift and press the iron down as this stops the fabric stretching out of shape. Pressing also sets the stitches and puts the excess fabric in the seams where you want it. Do not open your seams, keep them closed and press them to one side of the stitching. Make a choice and stick with it – left or right. Or if one fabric is pale and one dark, press the seam allowances so they lay behind the dark fabric and don't show through.

Piecing

To match seams accurately when joining rows of patchwork together, push a pin at a right angle ¼in (6mm) down from the top edge of the fabric through the stitches of both seams, fixing the pin vertically down the seams to be matched (Fig 6). The seams should align, but if they don't you can always un-pick them and try again. Or just leave them mismatched and move on!

APPLIQUÉ

Appliqué means 'applied to' and usually refers to a fabric image applied to a background fabric. You can use most appliqué methods for the projects in this book, however if you want to use traditional needle-turn appliqué you will need to add seam allowances to the shapes first. I used fusible appliqué and free-motion stitching for all the projects, so the following instructions describe that technique.

You may find it easier to photocopy the templates in this book, but please do this only for your own personal use. If you want you can make them bigger or smaller too. The templates are reversed in the book, so when they are traced and ironed onto the fabric they are facing the correct way. The following instructions are specifically for a fusible web called Bondaweb, so please double check the application instructions for your fusible web brand before beginning. Once fused, the shapes can't be moved without leaving a sticky residue on the fabric and once cool they can't be removed at all.

Fig 6

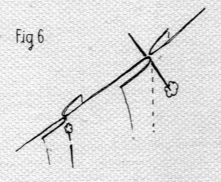

Fusible web appliqué

1 Lay a piece of Bondaweb (paper side up) over the template and trace with a sharp pencil or pen (see picture 1). Every piece of the subject you want to be in a different fabric has to be traced separately.

2 Cut the shapes out with paper-cutting scissors leaving a small allowance all round. Place the shapes paper side up on the *reverse* of your chosen fabrics and iron to fix in place (2).

3 Cut the fabric shapes out as carefully as you can on your traced pencil lines (3).

4 Peel off the backing paper. If this is tricky, scratch the middle with a pin and peel it away (4). Position all the pieces in exactly the right place (tucking houses underneath roofs and so on) before finally ironing them down on the background fabric (5).

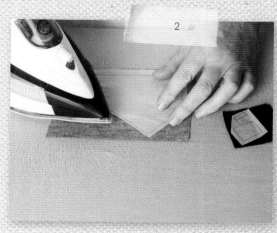

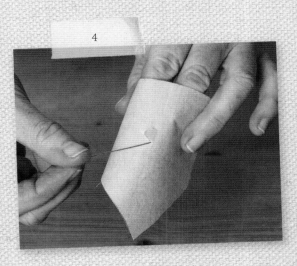

FREE-MOTION QUILTING

I have used free-motion stitching to secure the fused appliqué to the background fabric and to add detail and interest to the houses themselves. When you are free-motion stitching *you* and not the sewing machine determine the size and placement of each stitch. Good results take practice as you can imagine!

Set up your machine

Check your instruction booklet but for most machines you will need to lower the feed dogs and add a darning foot (see picture). Your machine will be happier free-motion stitching if it has a new needle. (Did you know you're supposed to replace the needle after every five hours of sewing?) I also select the 'needle down' position, so that when I take my foot off the pedal the needle stays in the fabric and I can have a little rest without losing my place. Not all machines have this facility though. Now, there's nothing else for it, you just have to start. It may end up in the bin, you may get a bobbin-y mess or a broken needle, but what does it matter?

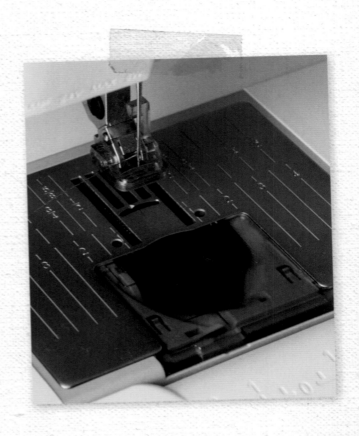

Free-motion pointers

- Remember that you (not the machine) must move the fabric and control the length of the stitches. If you were drawing with a pencil and paper, you'd move the pencil, but here you move the paper.

- Remember to pull up your bobbin thread rather than let it get tangled on the reverse.

- Look where you are going, not where you've been – it's too late for that!

- Don't press the fabric down, just guide it with your fingertips (see picture 1). And keep your fingers well away from the needle!

- Don't swivel the fabric round as you might if you were zigzagging around an appliqué, but keep the fabric facing the same way at all times.

- Try not to put your foot to the floor! A nice steady flowing speed is what you want. Keep your posture relaxed and open (2).

- If you are getting hundreds of tiny stitches the machine is going too fast and you are moving the fabric too slowly.

- If you are getting enormous stitches the machine is going too slowly and you are moving the fabric too fast. It really doesn't matter if all your stitches are the same length (mine certainly aren't) but the overall effect should be even.

- Remember that the fusible web has secured the appliqué to the background fabric, so your stitches can be more decorative than functional.

- Life is too short to un-pick free-motion stitching. So if you can, just throw your mistakes in the bin. Now, be nice to yourself and have an honest look at some of my stitches in the book – they're not all perfect either are they?

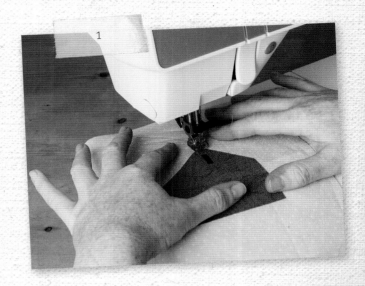

EMBROIDERY

Tracing templates onto fabric

I use a water-soluble pen to mark up embroidery or quilting patterns onto fabric. If the fabric is hard to see through when tracing hold the template and the fabric up to a window and trace them that way. If you still can't see the template, trace the design onto a removable paper (such as Stitch 'n' Tear) and embroider or quilt through that, removing the paper carefully at the end.

Needles and threads

Your needle needs to be sharp enough to pull through the fabric comfortably, with an eye just big enough to hold the thread. If you use a needle with a very large eye and a thinner thread you will be left with holes in your work.

Threading a needle

- Always thread the needle whilst the thread is still on the reel as this prevents the end fraying (Fig 7).

- Measure the thread on your forearm and cut it at your inside elbow. Any longer and the thread will just twist round and round itself and get tied into knots.

- Cut the end of the thread on the diagonal as it will then thread through the eye of the needle more easily.

Fig 7

Fig 8

Running stitch

Running stitch (Fig 8) is the first embroidery stitch you should learn – you can use it for almost everything! Running stitch is also used for hand quilting.

1 Start with the fabric positioned so you can stitch comfortably from right to left. Thread the needle and knot the end of the thread. Bring the needle up from the back of the fabric and take a small stitch, pulling the thread until it lays flat on the surface without pulling the fabric out of shape.

2 With the needle still underneath the fabric leave a small space (the same size as your stitch) and bring the needle up and back down into through the fabric to form the next stitch. Repeat this process. Once you've practised it is quicker to put a few stitches on your needle before pulling the thread through.

Fig 9

Backstitch

Backstitch (Fig 9) is one of the simplest and most versatile stitches, forming a clear and solid outline.

1 Thread the needle with three strands of embroidery thread and knot one end. Come up through the fabric so that the knot is on the reverse of the work. You will be stitching from the right-hand side of the fabric towards the left.

2 Take one stitch to the right-hand side (backwards) and bring the needle back up another stitch length away to the left-hand side. Pull the thread through so it rests on the fabric but doesn't pull the fabric.

3 Now work backwards to meet the previous stitch, bringing the needle back up another stitch away. Continue in this way.

Satin stitch

Satin stitch (Fig 10) is used to add colour and to fill in a shape. Satin stitch uses a lot of thread and is best used in small areas.

1 Outline the shape to be embroidered in backstitch first to give a neat edge.

2 Working very neatly and trying not to twist the thread, put the needle up through the fabric on one side of the shape and down the other, leaving a flat, long stitch on the surface of the fabric.

3 Continue in this way until the whole shape has been filled in.

Fig 10

MAKING A QUILT SANDWICH

Layering up a quilt is the process needed to get all three layers of your quilt – the pieced quilt top, the middle wadding (batting) and the plain fabric back – together before quilting can begin. These three layers are called the 'quilt sandwich'. These layers, and the quilting stitches, will turn your patchwork into a quilt.

Preparing backing fabric and wadding (batting)

The quilt backing needs to be larger than the pieced top, so if your quilt is wider than the fabric you have chosen (and they generally are) you will need to cut two lengths of fabric and sew them together. Stitch the fabric lengths with right sides together and press with the seams open.

- Your wadding (batting) should also be larger than your quilt top. If your wadding has been kept tightly rolled or folded, lay it out flat for a while to allow it to relax and expand before using it.

Layering up the sandwich

1 Place your backing fabric right side down on the floor or a table. Pin or tape in place to keep the fabric as straight and flat as possible (Fig 11).

2 Carefully place the wadding (batting) on top of this and then add the pieced top right side up, keeping all three layers as straight and flat as you can.

3 The quilt sandwich needs to stay securely together whilst you are quilting it. This is achieved by tacking (basting) the layers together or by fastening them with curved safety pins. Tacking is just large running stitches. You should tack the sandwich for hand quilting and use safety pins for machine quilting. The quilt sandwich needs to be pinned or tacked horizontally and vertically in lines no more than a hand's width apart (Fig 12).

Fig 11

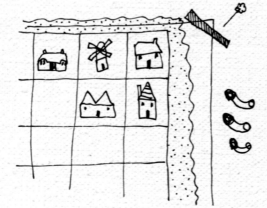

Fig 12

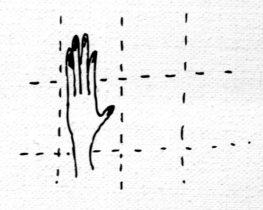

QUILTING

Quilting in its simplest form just keeps the three layers of the quilt together, but it is also used decoratively to add texture and pattern to the surface of the quilt. The more quilting you do the less warmth the quilt will provide. Quilting can be done by hand or machine.

Marking up a quilting design

I like to mark up (draw) my quilting design on the pieced quilt top before I layer it up ready for quilting. The quilting design can be traced using templates or a pattern, or it can be hand drawn. I mark up my chosen design using a water-soluble pen but you can use chalk or be very traditional and use an old, dry slither of soap.

HAND QUILTING

Hand quilting is simply small and evenly spaced running stitches that go through all three layers of the quilt sandwich to keep them together. Start from the centre of the quilt and keep stitching outwards, working in all directions equally (Fig 13).

Beginning and ending quilting threads

Knots used to start and end your quilting need to be buried out of sight inside the quilt sandwich.

1 Cut your quilting thread to no more than 12in (30cm) long, make a small knot in one end and then thread the needle.

2 Insert the needle away from (off) your drawn quilting line (Fig 14) and bring it up on your quilting line. Pull gently on the thread until you feel the knot bury itself in the wadding (batting). Do a backstitch and then continue with small even running stitches on your marked lines.

3 When you come to the end of your workable thread, make a small knot and 'bury it' off your quilted line into the sandwich as before.

Fig 13

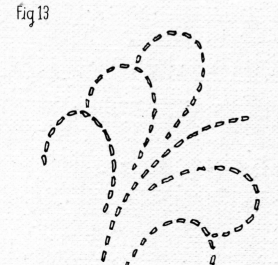

Fig 14

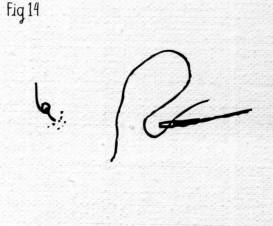

MACHINE QUILTING

Quilting by machine is obviously a lot quicker than hand quilting but it takes a little practice to achieve good results.

Machine quilting pointers

- It is very important to start machine quilting from the centre of the quilt. You will need to roll your quilt sandwich to position it under the sewing machine foot and keep the layers together whilst sewing to ensure a flat and neat result. You can keep the roll together with a bicycle clip (Fig 15).

- Select a slightly longer stitch length on your machine and a stronger machine quilting thread.

- Remove the safety pins as you approach them and be careful to work outwards from the centre of your quilt in all directions equally.

- You will need to secure your threads at the start and finish of your quilting lines by taking a backstitch and burying the ends as you would for hand quilting.

Long-arm quilting

You can pay for a long-arm quilter to layer up and quilt your patchwork for you. Most quilts shops will be able to recommend a long-armer. They stitch continuous flowing lines all over your quilt with a special computerized sewing machine that works in a long frame.

Fig 15

BINDING

The raw edges of quilts are finished by adding a binding. This is a narrow strip of fabric sewn over the raw (un-finished) edges of your quilt sandwich, completely encasing, strengthening and neatening them at the same time. Choose the fabric for the binding when the quilt is finished, just as you would chose a picture frame. The instructions that follow are for a continuous binding with mitred corners, which will act as a beautiful frame for your quilt.

Making binding

You will need to prepare sufficient binding to go all around your quilt plus about 8in (20cm). Cut your fabric into strips 3in (7.6cm) wide and sew together into one long piece (Fig 16). Press the seams open. Now press the binding in half lengthways with wrong sides together.

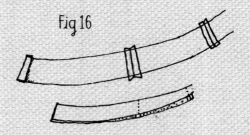

Fig 16

Stitching the binding

1. Trim the excess quilt backing and wadding away so the edges are straight and even. Start in the centre of the right-hand edge of the quilt with the top (right side) facing you. Align the raw edges of the binding with the quilt raw edges and pin in place leaving an 8in (20cm) tail (Fig 17).

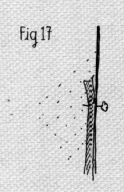

Fig 17

2. Stitch with a ¼in (6mm) seam allowance, stopping ¼in (6mm) away from the first corner and making a double stitch to strengthen this point.

3. Take the quilt out of the machine. Fold the binding up to form a 45-degree angle and press with your nail (Fig 18). Fold the binding back on itself to align with the next edge of the quilt. This is a mitred corner. Double stitch in place starting from the top and continue stitching to within ¼in (6mm) of the next corner. Work each corner in this way.

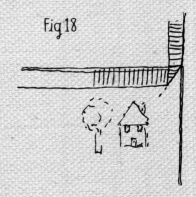

Fig 18

4. When about 8in (20cm) from the starting point, take the quilt out of the machine and adjust so that the start and end of the binding will overlap and lay smoothly on your quilt. Fold under the starting edge and overlap the bindings by tucking the finishing end of the binding inside it (Fig 19). The binding will probably be too long to lie neatly, so trim the excess away. Make sure the bindings lie neatly when sewn in place and pin to secure. Stitch in place.

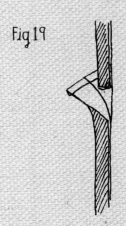

Fig 19

5. Fold the binding over to the back of the quilt. Slipstitch in place all round, with neat corner mitres.

FINISHING AND HEMMING

Slipstitch

Slipstitch is excellent for finishing hems and closing gaps in seams because the stitches are hidden inside the folds (literally slipped between) and are therefore barely visible.

1. Stitch from right to left. Knot your thread and bring it up from the back of the fabric a few threads away from the folded-up hem or the opening furthest away from you.

Fig 20

2. Using the point of the needle, pick up a thread or two of fabric from the opposite side of the hem or opening. Pull the thread through (Fig 20).

3. Place your needle again into the other side of the folded hem near your last stitch and run it through (inside) the folded hem a short distance. Pull the thread through the fold and out into the seam edge. With the point of your needle, take up another thread of fabric on the opposite hem, directly across from where the needle came out of the fold. Run the needle through the fold as before and repeat. You will have made very small, barely visible stitches and all the travelling threads between them will be hidden in the folds.

Hemming

A hem is the folded edge of a piece of fabric that is sewn down to neaten the edge and to prevent it fraying (Fig 21). Fold up the raw edge of the fabric and press. Fold up again and stitch in place either by hand using a slipstitch or by machine.

Fig 21

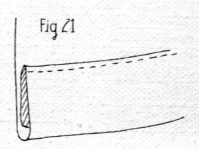

FRAMING

I use several framing methods to finish and present my appliqué. The one you choose will depend on how much wall space you have and how protected from the elements the picture needs to be.

Framing behind glass

This is the simplest method as you only have to do a spot of shopping!

1. Find a frame you like that will comfortably hold the appliqué. You could paint the frame if you want to. Cut the mount board to the same size as the frame measurements.

2. Attach glue dots to the top edge of the appliqué picture on the reverse. Carefully position your appliqué picture on the mount board so that it is in the centre of the width but slightly nearer the top of the board. Press the glue dots firmly in place.

3. Before framing you need to sign and date the mount board and clean the glass. I also dab some sticky tape over the appliqué picture to pick up any stray threads or hairs. Place the mount board in the frame and secure the backing. Hang the picture so the centre of the image is at eye level.

Making a Wooden Frame

I like to frame my appliqué pictures this way as it makes them stand off the wall. They can be propped on a shelf too. They're not protected from light and dust, so this method isn't suitable for every room.

1 Cut your wooden battens to the dimensions given in the appliqué picture pattern and make sure that the edges are at right angles and are not sharp enough to damage your fabric. Screw them together at the corners from the outside edge (see picture 1).

2 When your frame is made you can start stapling the picture to it. Start from the top centre and staple once, making sure the picture is in exactly the right place (2). Turn the frame upside down, pull the fabric taut and staple in place again, just once. Now staple once on each side and start the process again from the top centre, working around and out to within 2in (5cm) of the frame corners (3).

3 To secure the fabric neatly at the corners you need to imagine hospital corners on beds! Fold the fabric down so it is safely out of the way and trim the excess wadding (batting) from the corners to reduce the bulk and let the fabric sit as neatly as possible. Tuck one side of the fabric under the other, pulling it tightly so the corner is square, and staple in place (4). Repeat for all four corners.

LABELLING A QUILT

It is traditional to make a small fabric label to be sewn to the back of your finished quilt (Fig 22). This can note your name, the date you started the quilt and the date you finished it (often an embarrassingly long time apart!) and if relevant, the name of the quilt, the recipient and perhaps the occasion it was made for.

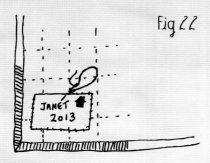

Fig 22

CARING FOR QUILTS

Folding quilts

Quilts should be folded with their best side outwards, because then the valley folds that will make permanent creases are in the back of the quilt. If quilts are kept folded it is important from time to time to open them and lay them flat for as long as you can, and then re-fold them in different places to prevent the valley folds becoming permanent.

Laundry

You can wash your quilts but it will age them so cleaning is best kept to a minimum. Spot clean little stains with soap or, if stubborn, a solution of baby sterilizing fluid, but check first to see if it will bleach the colours. Quilts can be machine washed and tumble dried if you are happy for them to look loved and crumpled. I am, so I do. Alternatively, take quilts to a dry cleaner. You can also put quilts in the freezer briefly to kill moths.

TEMPLATES

The templates are presented in book order whenever possible. Some templates are used for more than one project, so read the project instructions and template labels carefully. Templates are full size and are reversed where appropriate ready for fusible web appliqué.

Neat Town Houses Quilt

Number templates

Actual size

Reversed, ready for fusible web appliqué

House templates

Actual size

Street Skyline Quilt

House Templates

Actual size

Mix and match the house parts to create your own rows of houses

Street Skyline Quilt

Templates

Actual size

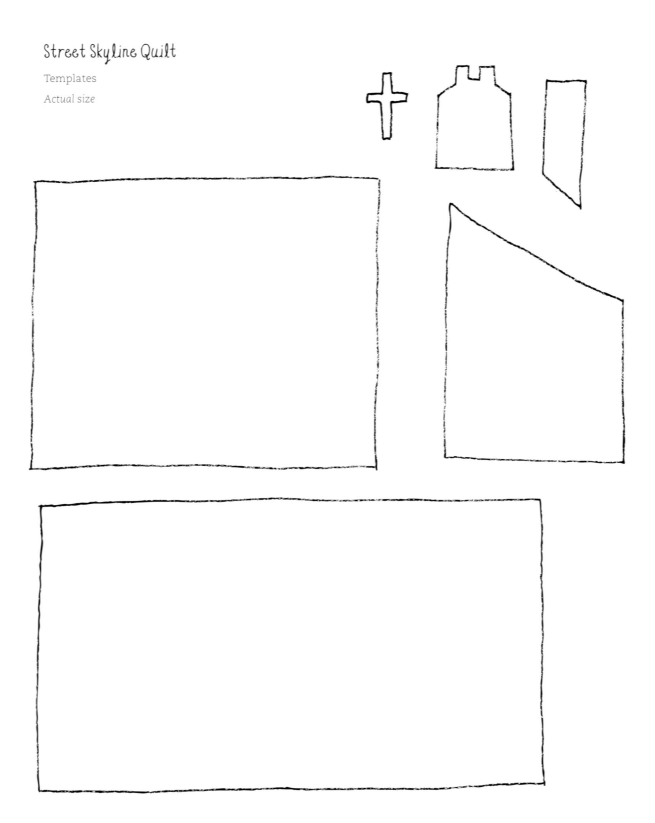

Detached Houses

House Layout Template

Actual size

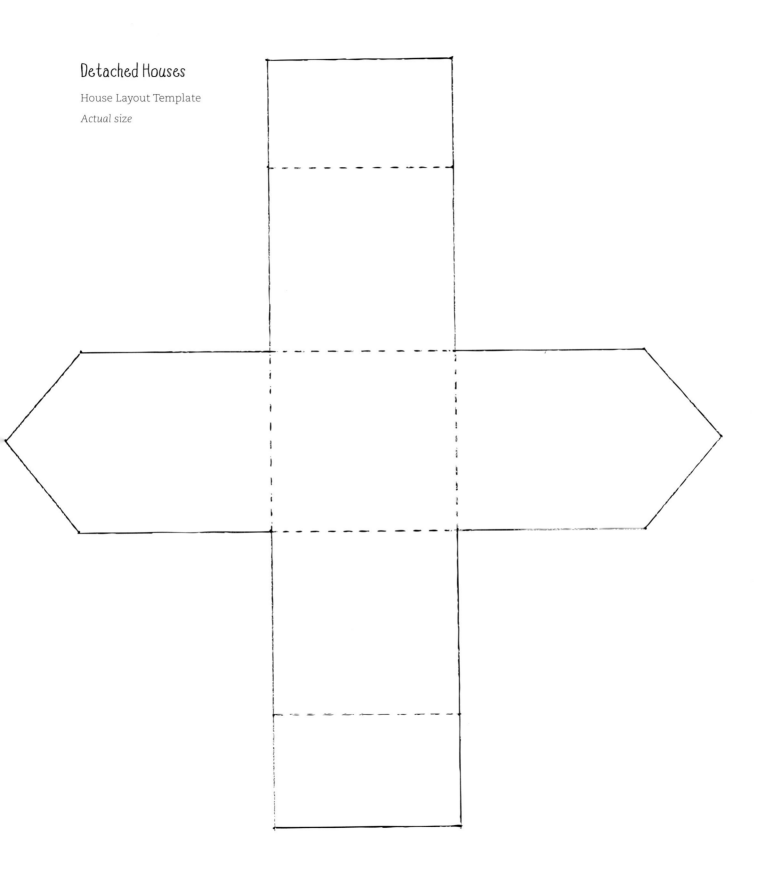

Village Squares Quilt and
Village Map Quilt

Templates

Actual size

Use this cottage template for the
Woodland Cottage Hanging too

Use this house template
for the Village Map Quilt

Village Squares Quilt and
Village Map Quilt

Templates
Actual size

113

Village Squares Quilt and
Village Map Quilt

Templates
Actual size

Use this bush template
for the Woodland Cottage
Hanging too

Village Squares Quilt and
Village Map Quilt

Templates
Actual size

Use the tractor and trailer
templates for the Village
Map Quilt

Village Squares Quilt and Village Map Quilt

Templates
Actual size

Little bird used in the
Village Map Quilt

Village Squares Quilt and Village Map Quilt

Templates

Actual size

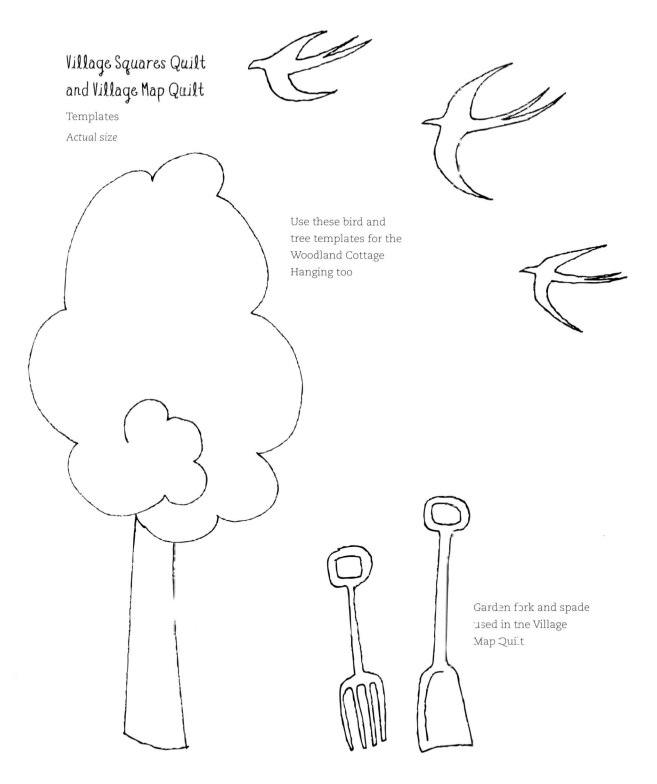

Use these bird and tree templates for the Woodland Cottage Hanging too

Garden fork and spade used in the Village Map Quilt

Country Lane Table Runner

Templates

Actual size

118